Sir Arth...

The Final P~~roblem~~
and Other Stories

Adaptation and activities by **Eleanor Donaldson**

Illustrated by **Fabio Visintin**

Series Editor: Robert Hill
Editor: Daniela Difrancesco
Design and art direction: Nadia Maestri
Computer graphics: Carlo Cibrario-Sent, Simona Corniola
Picture research: Alice Graziotin

© 2013   Black Cat, Genoa, London

First edition: January 2013

Picture credits: Istockphoto; Dreams Time; Shutterstock Images: Hulton Archive/Getty Images: 4; De Agostini Pictures Library: 34; Hulton Archive/Getty Images: 35; Popperfoto/Getty Images: 36; © WARNER BROS/Web Photo: 66; Rue des Archives/Tips images: 82; Tips Images: 83; Cinetext/Allstar/Warner Bros/Tips Images: 84.

All rights reserved. No part of this book may be reproduced, stored in a retrieval system, or transmitted, in any form or by any means, electronic, mechanical, photocopying, recording or otherwise, without the written permission of the publisher.

We would be happy to receive your comments and suggestions, and give you any other information concerning our material.
info@blackcat-cideb.com
www.blackcat-cideb.com

Member of CISQ Federation
RINA
ISO 9001:2008
Certified Quality System

The design, production and distribution of educational materials for the Black Cat brand are managed in compliance with the rules of Quality Management System which fulfils the requirements of the standard ISO 9001 (Rina Cert. No. 24298/02/S - IQNet Reg. No. IT-80096)

ISBN 978-88-530-1329-3   Book + CD

Printed in Italy by Litoprint, Genoa

Contents

Sir Arthur Conan Doyle   4

A SCANDAL IN BOHEMIA   7
Part **ONE**   Holmes Receives a Visitor   9
Part **TWO**   The Marriage Ceremony   17
Part **THREE**   The Photograph   26

THE DISAPPEARANCE OF LADY FRANCES CARFAX   37
Part **ONE**   Watson Investigates   39
Part **TWO**   The Honourable Philip Green   48
Part **THREE**   An Unusual Coffin   57

THE FINAL PROBLEM   65
Part **ONE**   A Criminal Mastermind   67
Part **TWO**   A Narrow Escape   76
Part **THREE**   The Reichenbach Falls   86

DOSSIER   The Role of Women in Victorian England   34
                    Sherlock Holmes in Popular Enterteinment   82

ACTIVITIES   8, 14, 22, 25, 31, 38, 44, 46, 55, 62, 66, 72, 85, 91

AFTER READING   94

PET Cambridge PET-style activities   14, 15, 31, 53, 54, 62, 64, 73, 80, 85, 91, 92

T: GRADES 5/6 Trinity-style activities   14, 63, 81

These symbols indicate the beginning and end of the passages linked to the listening activities.

Sir Arthur *Conan Doyle*

Sir Arthur Conan Doyle was born in Edinburgh, Scotland, in 1859. He was the second son in a family of ten children. When he was nine years old, his uncles paid for him to study at a school in England. He later returned to Edinburgh to study medicine.

One of Conan Doyle's first jobs was as a doctor on ships and he travelled to the Arctic and Africa. After he returned to England, he opened his own doctor's surgery [1] in Southsea, near Portsmouth. He used the time that he spent waiting for his patients to start writing his first stories. Eventually, Conan Doyle stories were so successful that he became a full time author.

In 1885, Conan Doyle married Louise Hawkins, the sister of one of his patients. They had two children. Sadly, Louise died of an illness called tuberculosis in 1906. Later, Conan Doyle married again and had three children with his second wife, Jean Elizabeth Leckie.

Today Conan Doyle is probably best known for the Sherlock Holmes stories. The character of Sherlock Holmes was very similar to Conan Doyle's old professor, Joseph Bell. The professor once showed the class how to give an explanation for a patient's illness by using 'clues' [2] similar to those used by a detective and by observing a patient's everyday life and, for example, their job and past history.

1. **surgery** : the place where a patient goes to see a doctor.
2. **clues** : things to help you solve a problem.

Holmes and his assistant, Dr Watson, first appeared in *A Study in Scarlet* in *Beeton's Christmas Annual*, a popular Victorian magazine with stories, sold before Christmas each year. This was followed by a Sherlock Holmes novel, *The Sign of Four*, in 1890. Conan Doyle also wrote a series of short stories for a monthly magazine, *The Strand*. The stories were so successful that Conan Doyle found it difficult to be recognised for the other books he wrote. In 1893, he decided to end the series when he wrote *The Adventure of the Final Problem*, but when more than 20,000 readers stopped reading *The Strand* magazine, Conan Doyle finally wrote another story, *The Hound of the Baskervilles*. (This was written as if the story happened earlier than *The Adventure of the Final Problem*.) In a further collection of stories, beginning with *The Adventure of the Empty House*, Conan Doyle describes how Holmes escaped alive from his previous meeting with his rival, Professor Moriarty.

Conan Doyle is also the author of the fantasy novel *The Lost World* (1912). In *The Lost World*, the imposing [3] Professor Challenger goes on an adventure to South America and finds that dinosaurs are still living there. Professor Challenger was also based on a professor at Edinburgh University, William Rutherford.

Conan Doyle was given the title 'sir' for his work in a hospital during the Boer War in South Africa. Later he became very interested in life after death and unusual experiences. He spent a lot of time researching, just like he did in all his work, and he even wrote a book to try to prove that fairies [4] exist. This seems unusual for a man who used logic and rational thought in many of the things he did, but it is thought that the death of his first wife Louise and his father was a possible reason for his interest in these subjects.

3. **imposing**: looking important and big in appearance.
4. **fairies**: small imaginary beings of human form that have magical powers. They are often represented as small people with wings.

1 Comprehension check

Match the sentences (1-6) with the endings (A-F). Number the sentences in the order you read about them in the text.

1 The character of Professor Challenger first appears
2 Conan Doyle married twice,
3 Sir Arthur Conan Doyle was born in Edinburgh,
4 He wrote a popular series of Sherlock Holmes stories
5 His interest in life after death
6 He first started writing in his surgery

A ☐ possibly came as a result of the deaths of his first wife and his father.
B ☐ for *The Strand* magazine.
C ☐ while he was waiting for his patients to arrive.
D ☐ to Louise Hawkins and to Elizabeth Jean Leckie.
E ☐ where he also studied at university.
F ☐ in the novel *The Lost World*.

2 True or false?

What do you know about Sherlock Holmes? Decide which sentences are true (T).

Sherlock Holmes…

		T	F
1	wears a 'deerstalker' hat.	☐	☐
2	has a violin.	☐	☐
3	knows how to box.	☐	☐
4	wears disguises.	☐	☐
5	is married.	☐	☐
6	is also a doctor.	☐	☐

A Scandal in Bohemia

A C T I V I T I E S

Before you read

1 Definitions

Read this dictionary definition of the word 'scandal'. Where would you read or hear about a scandal?

'Something that shocks people because they think it is morally wrong.'

2 The set

In which European country is the area of Bohemia today?

1 ☐ Czech Republic   3 ☐ Romania
2 ☐ France   4 ☐ It doesn't exist.

3 Vocabulary

The words in the box are connected with criminals and crime solving. Use a dictionary to help you complete the table with the words given and the missing nouns or verb in its full form.

theft   investigation   kidnap   murderer   detection   rob

Noun	Noun (person)	Verb
theft	thief	to thieve

4 Listening

Listen to the first part of the story and answer the questions.

1 Who is telling the story?
2 What is a magnifying glass?
3 Is Sherlock Holmes in love?

PART **ONE**

Holmes Receives a Visitor

To Sherlock Holmes she is always the woman. I have not heard him speak about her by any other name. I can't imagine he felt an emotion like love. Feelings were excellent for uncovering motives but for the world's only consulting detective, an emotion like love was like a scratch[1] on his magnifying glass; it was a weakness in his perfect reasoning. There was no doubt, however, that one woman stood above all others in his eyes and that woman was Irene Adler.

For a number of years, I lived happily at 221B Baker Street with Sherlock Holmes. I often thought of calling to see him but since my move to a new house, and my recent decision to return to work as a doctor, I knew no more of Holmes's life than anyone else.

1. **scratch** : a cut with a sharp object.

PART ONE

One night, I was returning home after visiting a patient when I passed by my old rooms. I could see Holmes in the window. I watched as he walked up and down the room with his hands behind his back. Sometimes he paused, his fingers pressed to his lips in deep thought. I knew Holmes well from my experience of living with him. These were all signs that he was thinking about a case. I had some free time and I was interested to know more. The landlady, Mrs Hudson, welcomed me and led me into the sitting room. Holmes did not greet me, instead he pointed towards an armchair. He remained standing and observed me closely from the fireplace.

'Doctor Watson, it's good to see you looking so well. You are at least seven and half pounds heavier. You are working as a doctor again, I see.'

'Really, Holmes!' I exclaimed. 'But how did you guess?'

'And I see that your maid is careless...' he continued.

'Yes, you're also right about my maid. But how do you know all this?'

'My dear Watson,' he said. 'There are six scratches a few centimetres apart made by the brush your maid has used to clean the inside of your left shoe. Your maid has not done a good job because she is careless. The dot of yellow powder on your jacket is iodoform. [2] And I can see the mark where you keep your stethoscope [3] in your hat. From these observations, I note that you've clearly returned to work as a doctor.'

'Amazing!' I exclaimed. 'Yet when you explain it, it seems so obvious.'

2. **iodoform**: a powder once used by doctors to stop people feeling pain.
3. **stethoscope**: doctors use this to listen to your heart.

'That's because you see things but I observe things. How many times have you walked up the steps to this room?'

'Hundreds,' I replied.

'And how many steps are there?'

'I don't know.'

'Exactly! You see the steps but you haven't observed them. There are seventeen steps. Here — since you are interested in improving your observation skills, take this piece of paper and tell me what you think of it.'

He gave me a letter written on thick, pink note paper. I started to read aloud:

> At a quarter to eight a gentleman will visit you about an important matter. We have received good reports of your recent services to the Dutch Royal Family. We trust you can keep a secret, but do not think it strange if the visitor wears a mask.

'There's no date and there's no signature,' I commented. 'The writer is wealthy. It's expensive paper — it's unusually strong.'

'Precisely, Watson. That's the word: it's unusual. Now, hold it to the light!'

I could see letters printed into the paper. I read: 'E-g.'

'It's the symbol of the paper company,' I suggested.

'Not only that,' said Holmes. 'The letters show us the exact location of the paper company.'

He took an atlas[4] from his bookshelf.

'E... g... Eglow, Eglonitz... No, here it is! Egria, in Bohemia, famous for its glass and paper companies.'

He paused for a moment. I heard the sound of a horse and carriage arriving. Holmes looked out of the window.

4. **atlas**: a book showing maps and places.

PART ONE

'Those carriages cost several thousand pounds each,' he noted. 'There's money in this case, even if there's nothing else.'

'I should leave,' I said.

'No, you should stay. I might need your help.'

There was a loud knock at the door. The man who entered had an air of authority about him. He was six foot tall and had a wide chest. He wore heavy gold jewellery and a deep blue coat with a fur collar. His clothes looked expensive but they were not fashionable in England.

'Can I trust this man?' he asked Holmes, looking at me.

'You can speak to both of us or neither of us,' Holmes replied.

'Then I will begin. I am Count Von Kramm of Bohemia,' began the visitor in the mask. 'I should repeat that this concerns a very important matter which the king himself is worried about.'

Holmes looked bored.

'It is about a scandal of such importance that it could change European history,' he continued.

'If you could explain your case to me, Your Majesty, then maybe I can help you more easily.'

Surprised by the comment, the man took off his mask.

'Oh, why should I hide it from you! You are an excellent detective, just as I was told! Yes, the king has not sent me. I, Wilhelm Gottsreich Sigismond von Ormstein, am the King of Bohemia. Five years ago I met a lady. Maybe you know of her. Her name is Irene Adler.'

'Adler...' Holmes thought for a moment. 'Now, how do I know that name?'

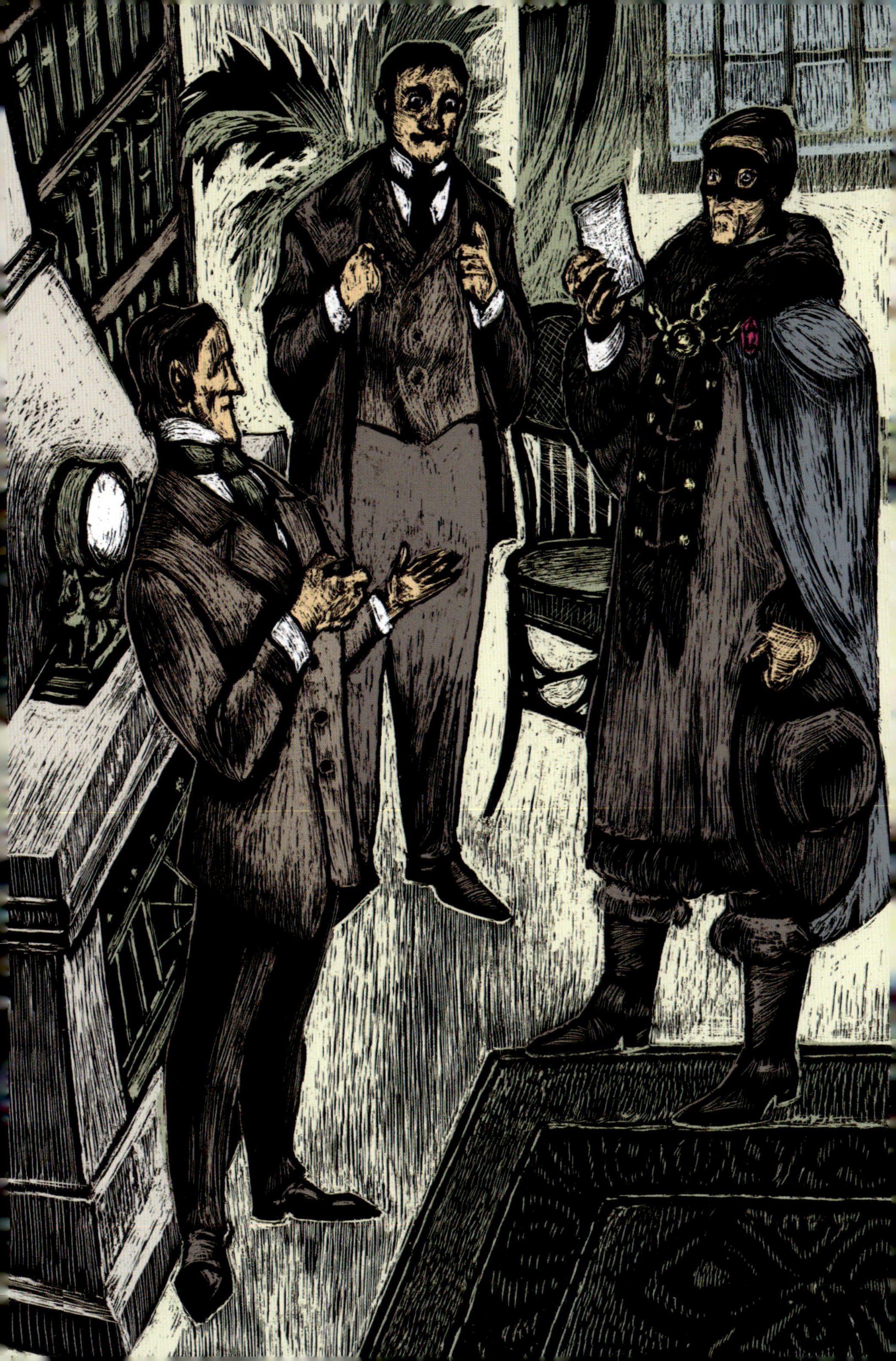

The text and **beyond**

PET ❶ Comprehension check

Decide if each sentence is correct or incorrect. If it is correct, mark A, if it is incorrect, mark B.

		A	B
1	Watson said Holmes loved only one woman.	☐	☐
2	Holmes used observation to find the answers.	☐	☐
3	Holmes thought the carriages looked old.	☐	☐
4	The visitor arrived wearing a mask.	☐	☐
5	The visitor was a Bohemian nobleman.	☐	☐
6	Five years ago the visitor met a lady called Irene Adler.	☐	☐

❷ Interpretation

Choose the best meaning for:
'An emotion such as love was like a scratch on his magnifying glass.'

1. ☐ He hated scratches on his magnifying glass; he hated being in love.
2. ☐ Holmes found anything that didn't allow him a clear view annoying.
3. ☐ Love makes things bigger than they really are.

❸ The characters

Do you think Holmes is right when he says to Watson:
'You see things, but I observe things.'

❹ Reading pictures

Look at the picture on page 13 of Part One for two minutes. Turn the page so you can't see it. How much can you remember about it?

T: GRADE 6

❺ Speaking: fashion

The king's clothes are said not to be 'fashionable' in England. Answer the questions about fashion.

1. What clothes are fashionable in your country at the moment?
2. Which brands are popular?
3. Are famous or rich people always fashionable?

ACTIVITIES

PET 6 Bohemia

Read the text below and choose the correct word for each space. For each question, mark A, B, C or D.

Bohemia once covered a large area of central Europe (0) ..A.. the present day Czech Republic. By medieval times Bohemia was a mostly independent state ruled by a king and then by an emperor. Bohemia became one of the (1) ..... liberal countries in the Western world; its inhabitants spoke Czech, German and Latin and it was popular with traders. This changed in the 17th century, when their ruler wanted the inhabitants to change their religion; (2) ..... rule ended in a long war and many of the country's nobles were killed.

Today the (3) ..... is divided into smaller districts in the Czech Republic. Interestingly, the word 'Bohemian' does not (4) ..... describe someone from Bohemia. The word is of French origin and is often used to describe someone who is artistic, liberal, and lives independently of society's rules, for example, some artists, poets and writers.

0	**(A)** including	B using	C ending	D choosing
1	A not	B most	C worse	D too
2	A its	B her	C their	D his
3	A areas	B countries	C region	D places
4	A sometimes	B never	C lots	D always

Detective work

7 You want to become a consulting detective. Decide which skills you need. Take it in turns to interview another student for the job of consulting detective.

Student A: prepare questions. For example:

Can you give me an example of when you:
- *had to keep a secret?*
- *tried to solve a mystery?*
- *gave someone advice?*

Student B: prepare answers to Student A's questions.

ACTIVITIES

Before you read

1 Opera quiz
In Part Two, you will read about a lady who sings opera. Test your knowledge about opera with the quiz.

1 The person with the main female part is
   A ☐ the lead vocal.
   B ☐ the leading lady.
   C ☐ the first lady.

2 Which is the lowest singing voice for a female singer?
   A ☐ soprano
   B ☐ contralto
   C ☐ tenor

3 Where is La Scala opera house?
   A ☐ Milan
   B ☐ New York
   C ☐ Vienna

4 Compared to a musical, opera has
   A ☐ more costumes.
   B ☐ fewer characters.
   C ☐ fewer spoken words.

2 Vocabulary
The title of Part Two is 'The Marriage Ceremony'. Who do you think will get married? Write eight words connected with marriage and weddings. Example: *bride*...

16

PART **TWO**

The Marriage Ceremony

Sherlock Holmes picked up a newspaper from his desk. His visitor moved around the room uncomfortably while Holmes read aloud.

'Friday 23 April: Irene Adler sings at the Royal Opera House. A *contralto*... I see she has travelled. She sang at La Scala, Italy; she was the leading lady in an opera in Warsaw, and now she lives in London. Let me guess: you've met this lady before and she is keeping something you want returned to you.'

'That's true! She has some letters that I wrote to her,' replied the king. 'But how did you...'

'She can't prove[1] anything,' Holmes said.

'I wrote them on my private notepaper. I signed them with my signature.'

'Well, it might be that she copied your signature and she stole your paper. What else?'

1. **prove** : show evidence.

17

PART TWO

'She has a photograph of us together.'

'Now it becomes interesting,' said Holmes. 'Was it an official photograph — one of a large size with the photographer's mark on it?'

The king nodded in embarrassment.

'I'm afraid Your Majesty has been careless. Why don't you steal it?'

'I've tried twice. Even my best men can't find it.'

'Then you'll have to pay.'

'She won't sell,' replied the king. 'It's not the money...'

'What will the lady do with it then?'

'I am going to marry a Scandinavian princess. On the day our engagement[2] is announced Irene Adler will send the photograph to my bride and to all the newspapers. The royal family in Scandinavia will never agree to the wedding if there is a scandal. I think you know my family, Mr Holmes... This will ruin[3] me.'

'When is the engagement?' asked Holmes.

'In three days.'

'Then we have plenty of time!' Holmes cried. 'There are a few things I must do first. As to my expenses...'

To my amazement, the king put down on the table three hundred pounds in gold coins and seven hundred pounds in notes.

'I will give you anything you ask for if you find the photograph,' he said to Holmes.

'I hope we'll soon have some news,' replied Holmes. 'Good night, Your Majesty.'

It was exactly three o'clock when I returned to Baker Street the next day. Holmes was out so I decided to wait to hear his news.

2. **engagement**: an agreement to marry someone.
3. **ruin**: destroy, cause great damage.

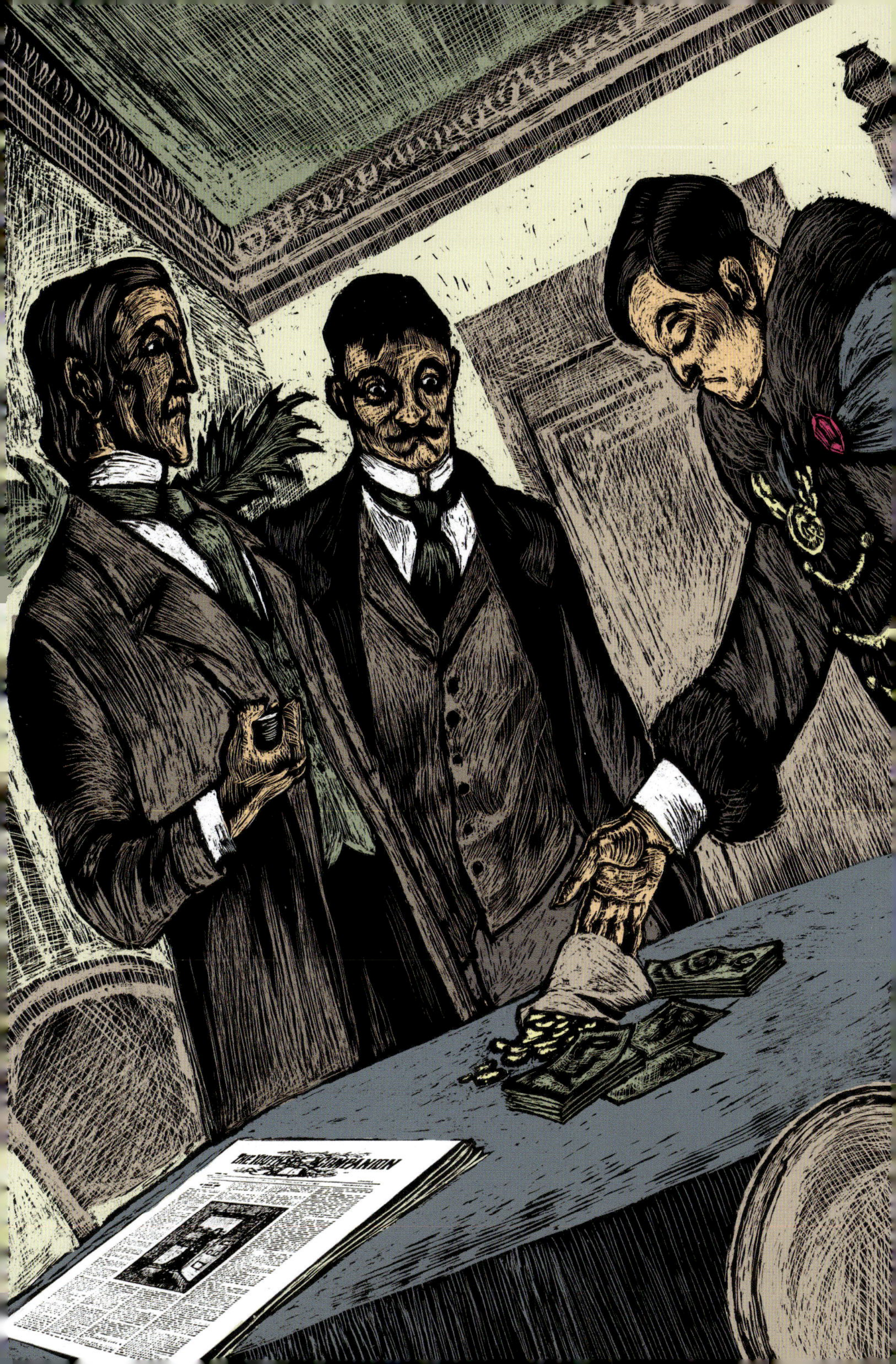
COMPANION

PART **TWO**

Nearly an hour later a stable groom [4] appeared at the door. He went straight into Holmes's bedroom.

'Surely that man can't be Holmes!' I cried.

Five minutes later Holmes was standing in front of me without his disguise. He laughed loudly.

'What's so funny?' I asked.

'Watson, you can't imagine the morning I've had,' he said.

'I imagine you went to Irene Adler's house.'

'Correct, but let me tell you what happened next. As you now know, I dressed as a stable groom looking for work. When I arrived at the house, I looked around to see if there was anything interesting. There was a large sitting room with the sort of comfortable furniture any respectable lady should have. It has long windows to the floor — a child could open the lock on them. At the side of her house, I found the stables. I asked if they had any little jobs. They allowed me to clean the stables. They also told me everything I needed to know.'

'And what did you find out?' I asked.

'Well, she doesn't go out much, except to her concerts. She rides into the park with the horse and carriage at five o'clock every evening and returns at seven for dinner. She has one male visitor and she sees him often. He's a lawyer called Godfrey Norton.

'When I left the stables a handsome man with a thin nose and a dark moustache arrived. I couldn't see Miss Adler, but I could see him through the large front windows waving his arms excitedly. He came out of the house and stopped a carriage.

'"Take me to St Monica's Church in Edgware Road," he said. "I need to be there in twenty minutes. I'll give you more money if you

---

4. **stable groom** : this person's job is to look after horses.

drive faster." Shortly afterwards, Miss Adler got into her horse and carriage. She asked the driver to take her to Edgware Road in less than twenty minutes.

'A moment later, I stopped a cab myself. The driver went as quickly as he could. Once we arrived, I followed them inside the church. The man turned around.

'"Come quickly!" he shouted to me. "We need your help."

'"Do you agree to witness [5] the wedding of Mr Godfrey Norton and Miss Irene Adler?" the minister asked. I looked at Miss Adler to be sure and said "yes". I watched as the minister carried out the ceremony and it all seemed perfectly legal.

'The lady was very grateful. She put a gold coin in my hand and smiled sweetly before the two of them left in different directions.'

Holmes paused for a moment and looked at the coin, which he now held in his hand.

'Why did they go in different directions?' I asked. 'You said they were married.'

'That's exactly what I thought, Watson, but at least we can continue with my plan. It's interesting — this marriage simplifies things.'

'How?' I asked.

'Miss Adler won't want her husband to see the photograph... unless he is, in fact, her lawyer. No, I don't think she would trust something so important to her to someone else. It's too large to keep with her. Tomorrow, we'll go to the house. I'll need your help.'

'But how will you find the photograph?'

'She will show me,' was his reply.

---

5. **to witness**: to sign a document saying that something took place.

A C T I V I T I E S

The text and **beyond**

1 Vocabulary

Choose the best option to complete each sentence. Put the sentences in order.

A ☐ Miss Adler's friend is *an opera singer/a lawyer*.
B ☐ The lady gives Holmes a *note/coin*.
C ☐ The king gives Holmes £300 in *gold/notes* towards his expenses.
D ☐ Holmes finds the *stables/keys* at the side of the house.
E ☐ Holmes finds out information from the *grooms/driver*.
F ☐ Holmes follows Miss Adler and Mr Norton to the *church/road*.
G ☐ Irene Adler has a *photograph/letter* that the king wants.
H ☐ Holmes is a *witness/priest* at Miss Adler's wedding.

2 Word square

Put the correct words from exercise 1 in the puzzle. Use the words in the red squares to complete Holmes's final sentence.

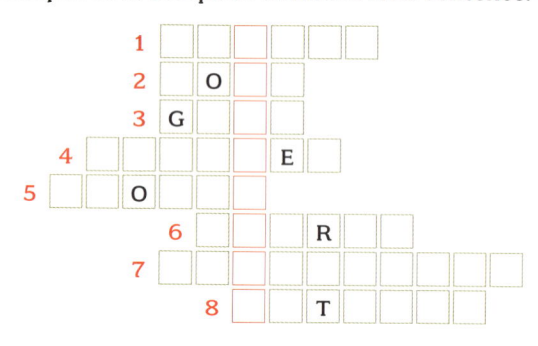

```
1 ☐☐☐☐☐
2 ☐ O ☐☐
3 G ☐☐☐
4 ☐☐☐ E ☐
5 ☐ O ☐☐
6 ☐☐ R ☐
7 ☐☐☐☐☐☐☐
8 ☐☐ T ☐☐☐
```

She .... me.

3 Vocabulary

Read the last line of the text in exercise 6, page 15 in Part One. Who do you think best fits the description of 'Bohemian' in *A Scandal in Bohemia*?

A ☐ The King of Bohemia   B ☐ Irene Adler   C ☐ Sherlock Holmes

22

ACTIVITIES

4 Celebrity gossip
Complete the newspaper article with the missing words.

fiancé	relationship	single	friend	restaurants

The Prince of Demark this week denied having a (1) .... with the German heiress Frieda Von Ormstein. The two have been seen at a number of (2) .... and nightclubs in Copenhagen in the past month. Friends said Miss Von Ormstein was a close (3) .... of the prince, but after having separated from her (4) .... Bruno Muller last year she wished to remain (5) ....

5 Interpretation
Read this quote from the English author Henry Fielding. Find the underlined part of the word in a dictionary and answer the questions.

'Love and scandal are the best <u>sweetene</u>rs of tea.'

1 What do you think Fielding meant?
2 Do you agree with him? Why? Why not?
3 Do you think the speaker likes talking about scandals?

6 Discussion
Discuss the questions with another student.

1 Are scandals always about love? Give some examples.
2 Do you think interest in celebrities or famous people is a good thing?
3 Are newspaper articles about other people's lives always true?

ACTIVITIES

Detective work

7 You are going to follow the people living in these houses. Describe the person/people that might live here and their daily routine.

I think a family lives here. They have a job that starts at nine o'clock and ends at five o'clock. On Sunday they do the gardening.

A

B

8 Which jobs do people do in Part One and Part Two that match the sentences 1-8?

This person...

1 makes people better.   ....
2 looks after horses.   ....
3 cleans and helps with the housework.   ....
4 understands and explains the law.   ....
5 investigates cases.   ....
6 can marry people in a church.   ....
7 uses their voice to entertain.   ....
8 rents rooms to people for money.   ....

ACTIVITIES

Before you read

1 Reading pictures

Look at the picture on page 27 and answer the following questions.

1 Describe the scene you see in this picture.
2 Who do you think is the man lying on the ground?
3 Who do you think is the lady by the door?
4 Why are two men running away?

2 Definitions

Do you know what a plumber's rocket is? Choose one from the following. Then check your answer on page 28.

A ☐ It is a smoke signal. It is used by ships at sea to let people know their location in an emergency.

B ☐ It is a smoke rocket used by plumbers. The smoke escapes and finds holes in water pipes.

C ☐ It is a fire cracker. It is similar to a firework. It was used in wars to create confusion.

3 Listening

You will hear the first part of Part Three. If the sentence is correct mark A. If the sentence is incorrect, mark B.

		A	B
1	The street was very quiet that night.	☐	☐
2	The men wanted money for their help.	☐	☐
3	A minister was hurt in the fight.	☐	☐
4	The lady did not want to help.	☐	☐
5	Watson threw an object through the window.	☐	☐
6	The roof of the house was on fire.	☐	☐

PART **THREE**

The Photograph

I arrived at Miss Adler's house at five to seven that evening. I understood that the lady's house was in a quiet street but, when I arrived, there were a lot of people there. One man stopped me and asked me for money. I refused.

Five minutes later, Irene Adler's carriage came around the corner. The men in the street ran towards it and started arguing about which one of them should help her out of her carriage. One man pushed the other and he pushed him back. The lady stepped out of her carriage and found herself in the middle of a fight. A minister came forward to stop the fight but he was hit in the face. He fell to the ground and hit his head on the pavement.[1] I could see blood. The men took one look and ran away.

'Is he dead?' asked one.

'No, he's still alive!' cried another. 'Miss, please help him!'

1. **pavement**: the place next to a road where people walk.

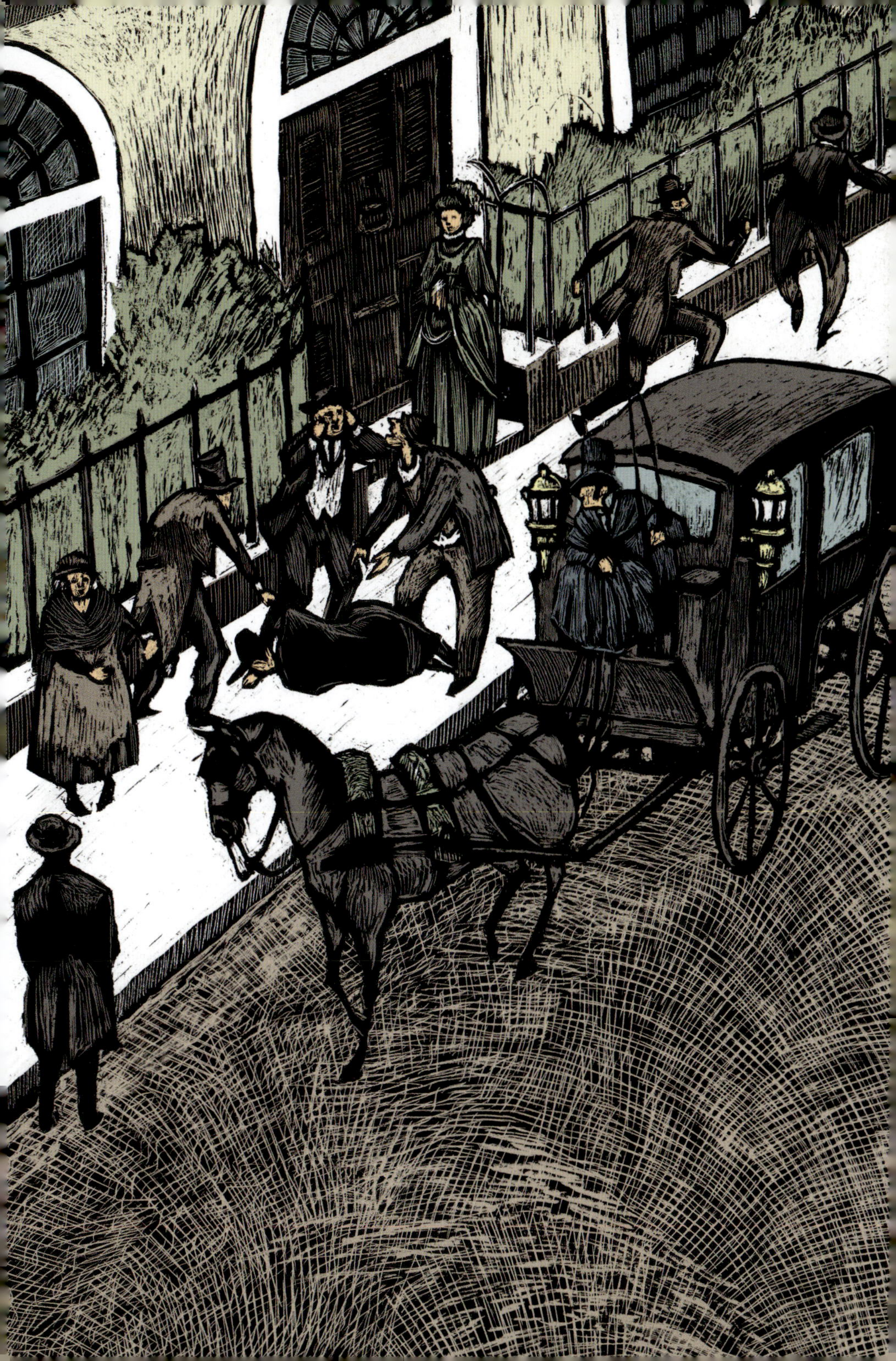

PART **THREE**

Miss Adler was standing near the door. Her dress caught the reflection[2] of the early evening light.

'Let him come into the house,' she said. 'He can't lie in the street.'

The servants carried him into the sitting room. I could see the minister lying on the sofa; he was talking to a maid. She went to the window and opened it, then he lifted up his hand. I took out from my pocket a plumber's rocket,[3] given to me by Holmes earlier that evening, and I threw it through the open window. I watched as smoke came out of the window.

'Fire! Fire!' I heard someone shout inside the house.

Soon the whole street was shouting: 'Fire!'

The smoke disappeared as quickly as it appeared.

Ten minutes later Holmes and I were walking towards Baker Street.

'Is everything alright?' I asked. 'It's lucky I knew about your disguise. For a moment I was worried.'

He showed me the 'blood'. It was red paint. Everyone in the street was paid as actors.

'You did a good job. The smoke disappeared in time for me to see exactly where the photograph is hidden.'

'I thought it was so secret that no-one could find it.'

'When there is danger, a woman with children picks up her child. A woman with no children looks for what she cares about the most. She went to get the photograph the moment she heard the word 'fire', but one of the stable grooms was watching me so I didn't get the chance to take it. At least we know where it is.'

'Where?'

'It's hidden in the wall. There's a secret button to open the place

2. **reflection** : an image that you can see in a mirror or in glass or water.
3. **plumber's rocket** : a smoke bomb used by plumbers to detect leaks in pipes before the era of pressure testing.

A Scandal in Bohemia

where the photograph is hidden. We'll go back tomorrow. She gets up at half past eight.'

When we arrived at Baker Street, Holmes stopped for a moment to take the keys from his pocket. A young man wearing a cap walked closely behind us.

'Good night, Mr Holmes,' he said.

Holmes turned around.

'I know that voice,' he said to himself, but the young man was gone.

I stayed the night at Baker Street. The next morning the king arrived early.

'So, do you have the photograph?' he asked impatiently.

'Not yet,' replied Holmes.

'Do you know where it is?'

'I do.' Holmes replied.

'Then we must go!' said the king. 'My carriage is waiting outside.'

'Irene Adler is married,' began Holmes.

'Married!' The king cried in amazement. 'How did this happen? Does she love him?'

'I hope for Your Majesty that she loves him very much. If the lady loves her husband, then she won't try and stop you from marrying your princess...'

When we arrived at Miss Adler's house, her maid was standing at the door.

'The lady left England at quarter past five this morning,' she said when Holmes introduced himself.

'She told me that you would come to see her.'

Holmes pushed past the maid and went into the sitting room. He pressed a button and there in a hole in the wall was a photograph, but it was not of the king. It was a picture of the lady, alone in her evening dress, and a letter addressed to Sherlock Holmes.

PART **THREE**

> Congratulations, Mr Holmes! You are indeed a very clever detective. Your disguises were excellent. Why wouldn't I help a poor old minister? I have heard a lot about you and I was sure that if the king was going to employ someone it would be you. I have worked in the theatre and so disguise is not new to me. Do you remember a young man last night? After you left, I followed you home before wishing you good night.
>
> Your client is safe. I have no interest in giving the photograph to the newspapers but I must protect my interests. A lady never knows what stories can be told and not all of them are true. My husband and I will stay in Europe for a while. I wish His Majesty success with his wedding. He may not have the photograph he is looking for but I have left another so he will remember me.
>
> Kind regards,
> Irene

'What a queen she would make!' cried the king. 'It's a pity we're not of the same class!'

'Oh, she is of a very different class to Your Majesty!' said Sherlock Holmes. 'That is certainly true!'

Fortunately the king didn't understand Holmes's meaning and continued excitedly.

'Thank you, Mr Holmes. This is a good ending for everyone! What should I give you for your services?'

'The photograph,' said Holmes.

'If that is your price, then it is yours,' said the king. He looked at it one last time before giving him the picture.

Holmes put the photograph in the inside pocket of his jacket. As far as I know, he has kept it since that day as a reminder of an incredible woman.

The text and beyond

PET 1 Comprehension check
For each question, choose the correct answer — A, B, C or D.

1 Why were there so many people in the street?
   - A ☐ They were all paid as actors.
   - B ☐ They were all looking for work.
   - C ☐ They wanted to see the famous Irene Adler.
   - D ☐ It was a very busy street.

2 What happened to the minister?
   - A ☐ He stopped the fight but was hit by the carriage.
   - B ☐ He was hit while trying to stop a fight.
   - C ☐ He hit his head when he helped the lady from her carriage.
   - D ☐ He hit one of the men but he fell to the ground.

3 When did Watson throw the plumber's rocket?
   - A ☐ When Holmes opened the window.
   - B ☐ When the maid opened the window.
   - C ☐ When the men shouted 'fire'.
   - D ☐ When he could see Holmes through the window.

4 Where was the photograph?
   - A ☐ In the far corner of the sitting room.
   - B ☐ Next to a secret button to open the window.
   - C ☐ Behind a secret bell near the window.
   - D ☐ Behind a secret opening in the wall.

5 Did they find the photograph the king wanted?
   - A ☐ Yes, it was left it in a secret opening in the wall.
   - B ☐ No, the photograph was a different one of the lady and the king.
   - C ☐ No, it was a photograph of the lady, but not with the king.
   - D ☐ Yes, she left the photograph but escaped with her husband.

6 Who was the boy that said 'goodnight' to Holmes?
   - A ☐ He was one of Irene Adler's servants.
   - B ☐ He was the stable groom who was following them.
   - C ☐ He was Irene Adler disguised as a boy.
   - D ☐ He was Irene Adler's husband, Godfrey Norton.

31

ACTIVITIES

2 Interpretation

Holmes says of Irene Adler: 'She is of a very different class to Your Majesty.' Which meaning did the king understand and which do you think Holmes meant?

A Her social level was different to the king's so they could never marry.
B Holmes had respect for Miss Adler but not the king.

3 Viewpoints

Choose a viewpoint, as in the example, and write a reply to the question. Why did Holmes put the photograph in his pocket?

Examples:

> *I don't believe Watson. Holmes did love Irene Adler, which is why his reasoning was not as good as it usually is. For example, he...*
>
> *Holmes will remember next time not to think than women aren't equal to men in their intelligence and capabilities. Irene Adler was able to...*

4 Cabinet cards

Read the information, then answer the questions.

Large photographs called cabinet cards were popular in the late nineteenth century. They were meant to be shown in a room so people could see them. The cabinet card was a photograph attached to a hard piece of card; the photographer advertised their business on the back.

1 Where do you think people usually kept the photographs described?
2 Why doesn't Sherlock Holmes think Irene Adler is carrying the photograph?
3 Where do you think Irene Adler is keeping the photograph?

'What a queen she would make!'

The modal verb ***would*** has many uses. Here are some of them:
1 to talk about desires that are not usually possible or real
2 to express the past form of 'will'
3 to politely make requests or invitations
4 to speak to about preferences, likes/dislikes.

32

ACTIVITIES

5 Would + infinitive

Number the sentences (A-D) with the example (1-4) in the box on page 32 that best describes how *would* is used in the sentences.

A ☐ Would you prefer tea or coffee?
B ☐ Would you mind helping me carry this?
C ☐ How lucky you would be to find a job like that!
D ☐ Last year, he said he wouldn't go.

6 Social networking

A social network is a type of 'meeting place' on a computer where you can share information in different ways. Imagine the messages between Holmes and Irene if they could write to each other using a social network and continue the conversation.

Irene:	*Excellent disguise, Holmes!*
Sherlock:	*Obviously not good enough...*
Irene:	*I like disguises ;-)*
Sherlock:	*...the boy last night?*

Detective work

7 The king wears a mask to disguise himself. Both Irene Adler and Sherlock Holmes use disguises. Discuss which of these things would be a good disguise.

fancy dress costume   pair of sunglasses   false moustache   hat   pipe

8 You are a detective and you need to choose the best disguise to follow your criminal. Choose the best disguise for the situation where the criminal:

1 always buys coffee at the same cafe.
2 tries to sell something they have stolen.
3 works as a professor at a university.
4 knows the coach in a football team.

The Role of Women in *Victorian England*

Queen Victoria: the ideal woman

As the 'mother of the nation', Queen Victoria represented the ideal woman. Queen Victoria seemed to enjoy the responsibility of married life and looking after the family. Her homes were fashionable and comfortable. She had nine children and a loving husband, the German Prince Albert, who was central to her happiness. When Albert died she went into mourning[1] for several years.

Marriage and children

A woman did not usually spend time alone with a man unless she planned to marry him. After she decided to marry, she had one partner: her husband. Marriage and children were important and many women married young. Society felt sorry for those women who didn't have children or remained unmarried as it meant an uncertain future. Although wealthy women had the advantage of financial assistance from their family, land or houses was often inherited by a male relative. In Victorian times, the family paid money to the husband as part of the marriage agreement but he still needed to have a good salary to give his wife a similar life. For a poorer woman, not

---

1. **mourning**: showing deep sadness over someone's death.

getting married might mean she had to look after relatives and do badly paid work either inside or outside the home.

Women in the home

A popular poem by Coventry Patmore at the time describes a woman as 'the angel in the house'. A woman's duty was to become a good wife and to look after the family. She should be patient, kind and unselfish. She should do everything to make her house comfortable and warm. A wealthy woman managed the house like a business. She checked payments to the servants and for things bought for the house. A middle-class [2] woman hoped to marry a husband who earned enough money so that she didn't have to work as well as manage a house. A poorer woman did not have a choice: she often had to work long hours as well as do the housework.

Women in work

Despite the ideal that women should mainly look after the home, information recorded during the mid to late nineteenth century suggests that thirty to forty per cent of women were doing some type of work. Although women could not have a business until the late Victorian period, many women still worked in a family business in some way, for example, by doing the accounts [3] or writing bills and letters. Professions open to women included working as a teacher in wealthy families – a position known as a 'governess' and later, nursing. [4]

2. **middle class** : a social group, neither rich or poor.
3. **accounts** : a record of money paid or received.
4. **nursing** : looking after people who are ill or hurt.

The biggest form of employment was as a maid, cook or cleaner. The next was in making clothes at home or a job in the growing number of factories, where women were usually the lowest paid workers.

Forms of entertainment, such as theatre and opera, were not considered a respectable form of employment for women because of the close contact with men. Many actresses were thought of as mistresses.[5] In *A Scandal in Bohemia*, Irene Adler is not considered 'respectable' but she still has her own money and a good life because of her relationship with the King of Bohemia. However, it is unlikely that she continued her life as a singer once she decided to marry.

Changes in the type of work women did came later on in the Victorian period, when women became part of political groups asking for changes in the law so they could have their own money and property. This also helped to change their role in society.

1 Comprehension check
Answer the questions.

1. What name was given to Queen Victoria?
2. Who often inherited property instead of a woman?
3. Describe the ways in which a wealthy woman ran her house like a business.
4. Give three types of work women did.
5. When did women's role in society start to change?

5. **mistresses**: women who have relationships with married men.

The Disappearance of Lady Frances Carfax

ACTIVITIES

Before you read

1 The characters

Read the title. Who is going to investigate in Part One?

2 Vocabulary

Match the words to the pictures.

1 boots   3 laces   5 knot
2 ticket   4 Turkish bath 6 travel agency

3 Comprehension

Read Holmes's description of Lady Frances Carfax on page 40. Answer the questions.

1 Is Lady Frances's father still alive?
2 Does she have her own money?
3 Who owns the family home?
4 Is she married?
5 Why do you think Holmes fears that something will happen?

PART **ONE**

Watson Investigates

I was sitting in Sherlock Holmes's rooms in Baker Street. He was looking at my boots.

'Why Turkish?' he asked.

'They're made in England,' I replied. 'I bought them yesterday.'

'I can see that!' he said. 'Anyway, I didn't mean your boots. I meant the bath. Why did you have a Turkish bath?'

'It's good for my health,' I said. 'I wanted a change.'

'You shouldn't let the assistants at the baths tie your boot laces. You tie them better yourself.'

I looked at my laces and saw the knot was in fact tied a little differently to the way I usually tied my knots.

'Incredible!' I thought. 'He notices the smallest differences!'

PART ONE

'If you really want a change, Watson, I have a job for you. You can go to Switzerland, all expenses paid. I have a case I must investigate there but I don't want to go too far away. Besides, I prefer my housekeeper's cooking to the food abroad. Mrs Hudson makes an excellent lunch, if you'd like to stay.'

'Thank you,' I replied. 'But I can't stop, I must go back home.'

Holmes ordered lunch anyway.

'I think Scotland Yard would prefer to see me in London,' he continued. 'There's one criminal in particular who will happily take advantage of my absence, but that is not something I can discuss at this moment.'

'I'd like to hear more,' I said.

'Lady Frances Carfax,' he began, 'the daughter of the late Earl of Rufton, is around forty years old. She is very beautiful for her age. She has the advantage of wealth and the disadvantage of having none of her own. Her brother owns the family home whereas she has no fixed address and no husband. She has some valuable Spanish jewellery, which she carries with her everywhere. I'm afraid that she may be in danger.'

'I don't understand,' I said. 'Is Lady Frances Carfax in Switzerland?'

'An interesting question,' he replied. 'Is she there or somewhere else? Is she alive or is she dead? Her family last heard from her more than five weeks ago. She has a friend in England she often writes to. She has had no letters from her.'

'Has anyone seen her?' I asked.

'She went into a bank in Switzerland four weeks ago and wrote a cheque for fifty pounds to her maid. Send me a telegram if you find out more information.'

Holmes gave me an address of a hotel in Lausanne.

The Disappearance of Lady Frances Carfax

'Holmes, are you really asking me to investigate?'

'Of course. Here — I have a first class ticket you can have! Now, shall we eat?'

Two days later I arrived at the hotel in Lausanne. I found out that Lady Frances often stayed there. She was a lovely lady. She was interested in books and she often went for walks on her own. She told the owner she was going to stay for the summer, but five weeks later she paid in advance and left early. The head waiter was engaged to her maid, Marie, and he knew nothing of their plans to leave until he received a letter from his fiancée. It said that she was visiting her family in France to tell them about their engagement. I asked to speak to him.

The waiter couldn't tell me much about Lady Frances. Marie never spoke about her employer's private matters but he remembered something interesting: in the last few days before she left, the lady seemed sad and worried. A dark-haired man with a beard was seen holding her by the arm near the lake. Marie thought the man was following her because she saw him again near the hotel. Soon after this Lady Frances left.

He gave me Marie's address in France and suggested I spoke to the travel agency in town.

The travel agency had copies of train tickets that were sold to two English ladies on the day they left. The final destination was Baden. The lady who paid did not leave her name and she did not leave an address for her luggage, which she preferred to keep with her.

In Baden, I found an English-speaking guest house. The hotel manager recognised Lady Frances from my description. Her maid only stayed one night. The lady was friendly with two guests,

PART ONE

Dr Shlessinger and his wife. Dr Shlessinger came to Baden to rest after becoming unwell during his time in South America. He was a very religious man and often spoke of his work with the missionaries there. Lady Carfax, in particular, seemed very interested in their missionary work and wanted to help. Dr Shlessinger paid for her hotel bill and the three guests said they were leaving for London.

'You aren't the only person looking for the lady,' the manager added. 'A man asked me about her. He was a big, bearded man. I think he was English but I didn't recognise his accent. I'd say he has lived abroad for some time.'

I was sure the man had something to do with Lady Frances's disappearance. I sent a telegram to Holmes to tell him how quickly I was resolving the matter and that I was leaving for France to speak with Lady Frances's maid. I received a telegram in return asking for a description of Dr Shlessinger's left ear. I didn't like Holmes's strange idea of a joke. I decided to continue with my investigations.

The maid lived in a small village and I quickly found her house. When I explained that her mistress was missing, she was very upset and told me everything I needed to know.

'I am so sorry!' she said. 'The mistress was angry at me for leaving and we argued. When I left she gave me a letter. There was a cheque for fifty pounds as a wedding present. She is such a kind lady but she has not been the same since she saw that man by the lake in Lausanne!'

'Which man?' I asked. 'Describe him to me.'

Just as she began describing the man, she screamed loudly at a face at the window.

'There he is!' she cried. 'The man I told you about! He's following us!'

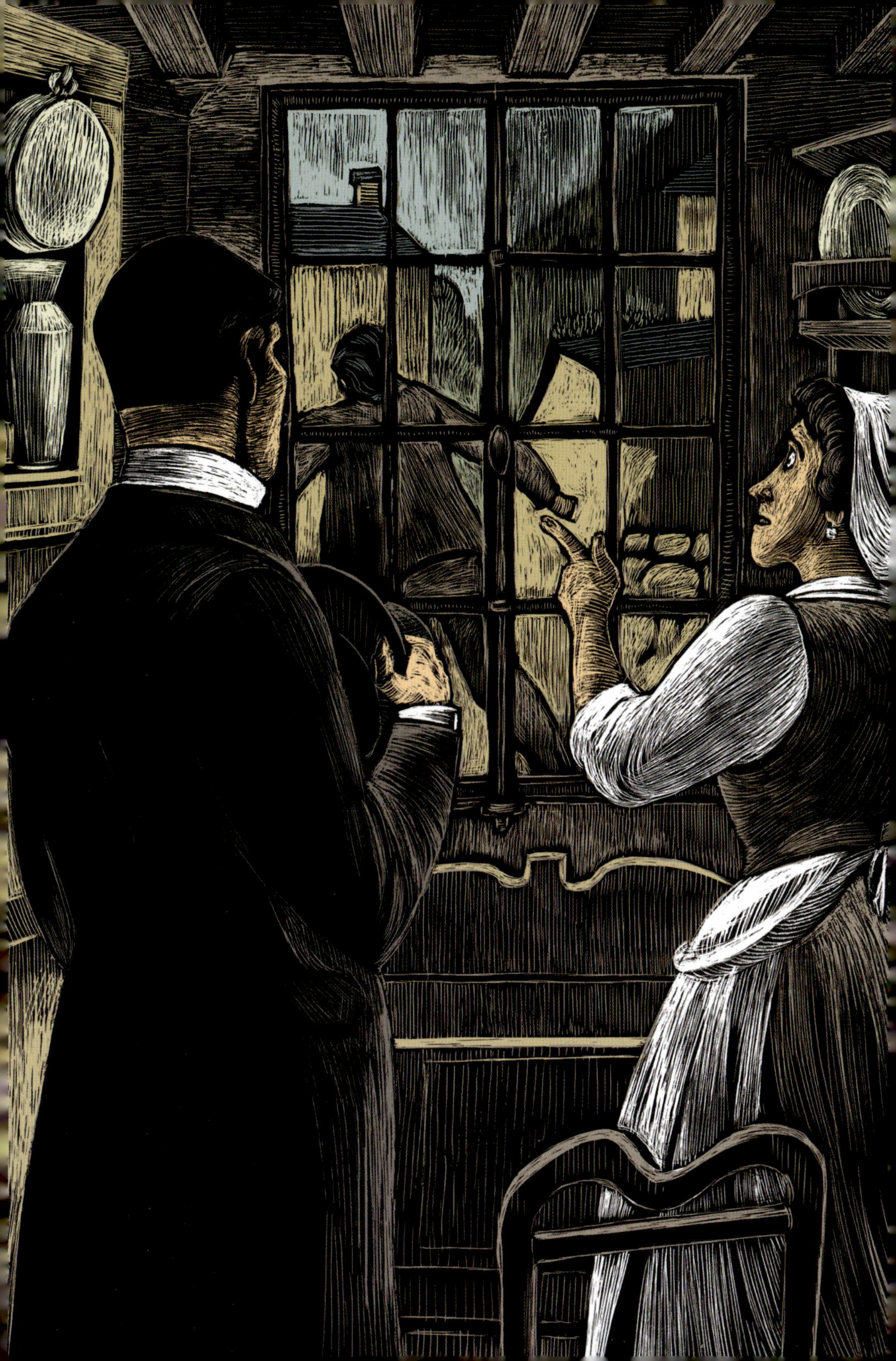

ACTIVITIES

The text and **beyond**

1 The past
Complete the clues (1-6) with a question word and the verb form in the past tense and match them to the correct answer (A-F). Rewrite the answers in full using the past tense as in the example.

What did Holmes say about Watson's boots?
He said that Watson shouldn't let the assistants at his baths tie his laces.

What	How much	Where	When	Why	Who

1 Holmes/say/about Watson's boots?
2 Lady Carfax/disappear?
3 Watson/go/first?
4 be/the cheque/to the maid?
5 Lady Frances's maid/go/to France?
6 Lady Frances/meet/in Baden?

A ☐ over five weeks ago
B ☐ Dr Shlessinger and his wife
C ☐ to tell her family about the engagement
D ☐ Watson shouldn't let the assistants at the baths tie his laces.
E ☐ fifty pounds
F ☐ to a hotel in Lausanne

2 Spot the difference!
Holmes 'notes the smallest differences'. Look at the pictures. Use some of the words in the box to compare them.

The boots in picture A have/are..., but in picture B... .

| buckle | laces | heel | sole |

A   B

44

ACTIVITIES

3 The characters
Who is this? Complete the sentences (1-5) with a person from the story.

1 .... has a valuable collection of Spanish jewellery.
2 .... was engaged to Lady Carfax's maid.
3 .... said Lady Frances left the hotel early.
4 .... paid for Lady Frances's hotel bill.
5 .... decided to continue his investigations by himself.

4 An email
This is part of an email you receive confirming your reservation at a hotel in Lausanne. Write a reply confirming the details.

From: info@hotellausanne.com

Thank you for your enquiry. We have a double room available for those dates. The cost for a standard room is 180 Swiss francs per night; the deposit is 90 francs. We also accept euros.

Please reply with the following information to make a room booking.

- Would you like an en suite room? (40 francs extra per room)
- Would you like to include breakfast? (16 francs per person)

We normally take the deposit by credit card (please supply details). Bank transfer details are at the bottom of this email.

5 A cheque
Lady Frances writes a cheque to her maid. Today many people transfer money between banks. Listen to the conversation between the cashier and the customer at the bank. Complete the details on the form with the information you hear.

Name (sender)	....
Account no	....
Recipient's sort code	....
Account no	....
Amount to be sent	....
Additional details	....

45

ACTIVITIES

'She told him to wait for her to return.'

If you want to tell someone else what a person said, instead of repeating their words in direct speech ('*Wait for me to return!*' *she said to him*) we can use reported speech. We follow the words told and asked with an indirect object, e.g. *me, him*.

When we use reported speech the present tense often changes to the past tense.

> '*Why do you want to find Lady Frances?*' *he asked.*
>
> *He asked me why **I wanted** to find Lady Frances.*

Note the difference in the word order and the pronoun (you → I).

6 Reported speech

Look at the conversation between the maid and the waiter. Rewrite the sentences in reported speech using the words asked and told.

The waiter (he) asked the maid (her) what the matter was.

Waiter: *What's the matter?*

Maid: *Lady Frances is afraid of something.*

Waiter: *What is she afraid of?*

Maid: *A man is following her.*

Waiter: *Who is he?*

Maid: *I don't know.*

Detective work

7 Imagine you are investigating the case. You want to interview some of the characters about the man at the lake.

1. Choose two people to interview.
2. Make a list of three questions you want to ask them.
3. Practise the interview with another student.

Q: *Why was he in Lausanne?*

A: *I don't know.*

ACTIVITIES

Before you read

1 The characters

Can you guess who the Honourable Philip Green is?

- A ☐ the man following the maid
- B ☐ Dr Shlessinger
- C ☐ a new character in the story

2 Vocabulary

Which of the pictures below show something you might find in an undertaker's?

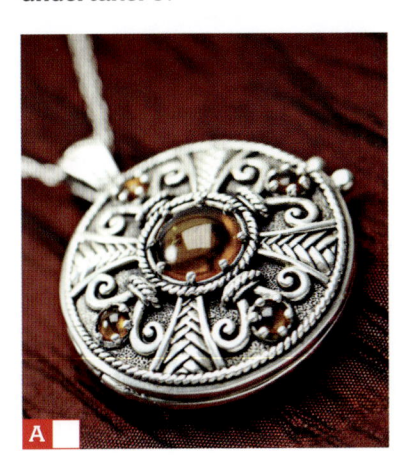

A ☐

B ☐

3 Definitions

Which meaning does the word 'honourable' have in the title?

- A ☐ a man with good intentions
- B ☐ a title given to the son of nobility

PART **TWO**

The Honourable Philip Green

I ran out of the door and down the street and there he was – he was a giant of a man! He was tall with wide shoulders, a dark beard and big dark-brown eyes. His skin was brown from the sun.

'Who are you?' I asked.

'Why do you want to know?' he replied.

'I'm looking for Lady Frances Carfax. She is missing. What have you done to her?'

'What have *I* done to her?' he repeated angrily. He put his hand on my throat and held it there until I couldn't breathe. I pushed him away but he held tighter. Then a man came running towards us from the cafe opposite.

'Stop!' he cried. He hit the bearded man on the arm and he let go of me.

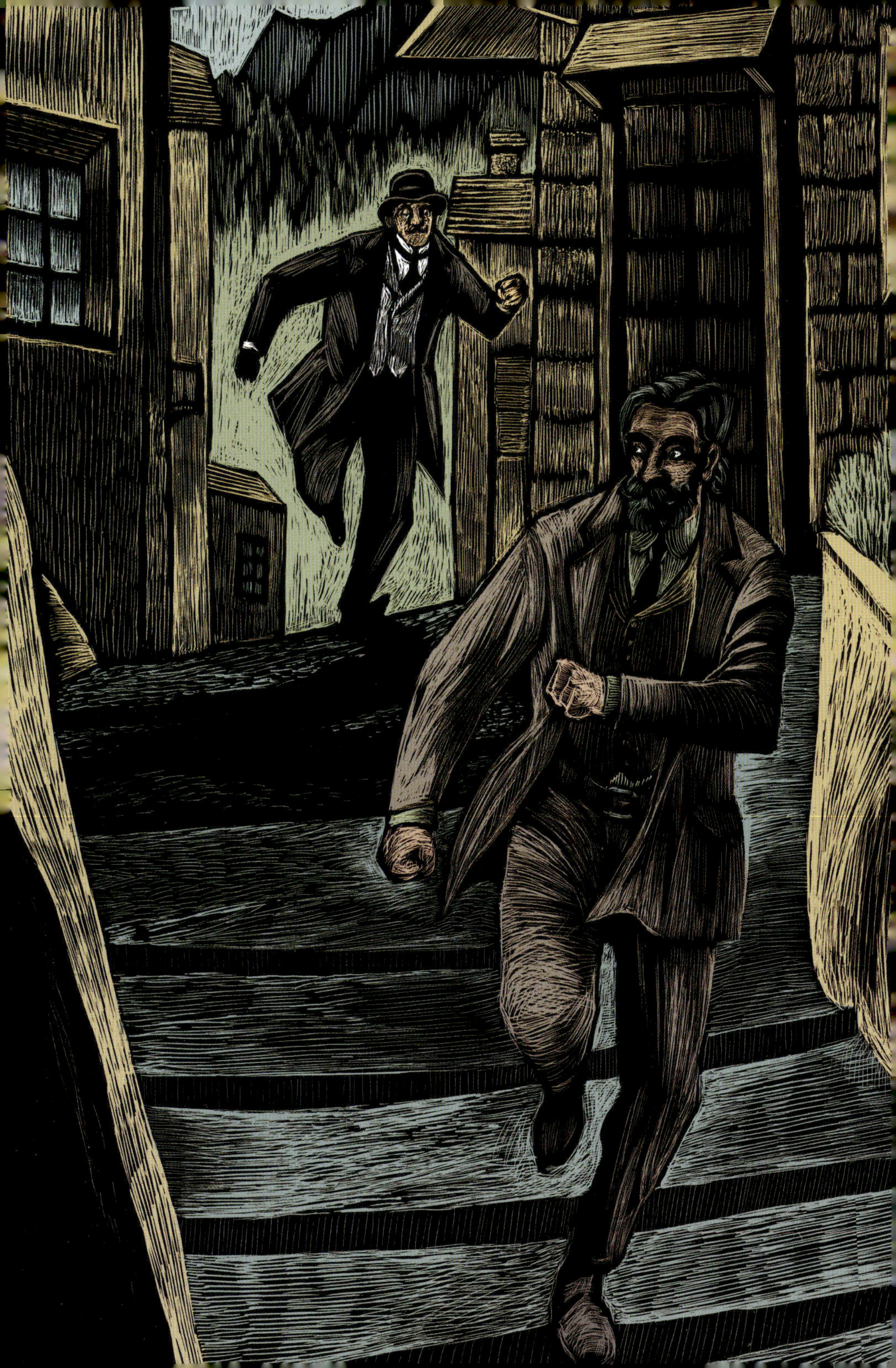

PART TWO

'It's lucky that I came,' he said. 'Is there anything you've done right in this investigation?'

I turned around and to my surprise I saw that the man was Holmes.

'You sent me here!' I shouted. 'I expect your investigations would be much better.'

'My investigations *were* better,' he replied. 'I found someone who can help us. And *you* started a fight with him.'

'This man is following Lady Frances's maid. He knows where Lady Frances is.'

'Good. Well, let's ask him politely,' said Holmes. 'Let me introduce you to the Honourable Philip Green, a family friend of Lady Frances Carfax.'

'I'm so sorry, sir! I'm losing my mind!' Green cried. 'I love Lady Frances more than anything. I don't know what to do!'

'Let's go back to the cafe,' said Holmes, 'and you can tell my friend Watson your story.'

'I've always loved Frances,' Green began, 'and I think she loved me. When I first met her I was young and stupid. She didn't think I was serious about her. Her father asked me not to see her again because she was going to get married, but now I know that wasn't true. I left for South Africa in the hope of making money there. I did well. I bought land and had a house with servants but I knew something was missing. Years later, friends told me that Lady Frances was still unmarried. I hoped it was because she still loved me. When I found her in Lausanne, she told me it was too late to think of marriage but I feel sure she still feels something for me! I thought perhaps her maid might talk to her. Now you tell me she is missing. Please, tell me, what has happened to Frances?'

'That is what I hope to find out,' said Holmes. 'I suggest you go

The Disappearance of Lady Frances Carfax

back to London. Send me your address. You can help us with our investigations.'

When we arrived in London the next day, there was a telegram waiting for Holmes at Baker Street. It said:

```
Left ear: torn, piece is missing
```

'What does this mean?' I asked.

'It's the question you didn't answer,' said Holmes. '"What does Dr Shlessinger's left ear look like?" Fortunately, I sent it to the hotel manager. He remembered.'

'I don't understand,' I said.

'Dr Shlessinger's left ear was bitten in a fight. He is better known to the Australian police by the name of 'Holy[1] Peters'. Mr Peters has spent years becoming friendly with lonely ladies who do good work. He tells them their money is for his religious work. One lady, who he calls his 'wife', left with him for South America. He stole from people who were dying. By the time the missionaries found out, they were on a ship to Europe. The longer Lady Frances stays with them, the more danger she is in.'

In a big city like London, Peters and his wife disappeared like they never existed. It was a week before one of Sherlock Holmes's contacts arrived at the door with information: a man wearing religious clothes and matching the description of Peters was seen selling an old Spanish necklace. The man looked pleased with the money he received and said that he had more jewellery at home. He would come back the next day.

On hearing this news, Sherlock Holmes asked the Honourable Philip Green to come to Baker Street.

1. **Holy**: devoted and religious.

PART TWO

'I must help!' Green said. 'I can't sit and do nothing.'
'Did you see a couple with Lady Frances in Baden?'
'Yes,' he replied.
'And did they see you?'
'No. I just followed. I didn't want to be seen.'
'Then, you must do exactly as I say. Tomorrow they will try and sell more jewellery. I want you to follow them. Come back here and tell me everything you see. Do not speak to anyone.'

The next day Green returned with the news.

'We've got him!' he cried excitedly. 'His wife sold another necklace an hour ago. I followed her down the street. She went to an undertaker. The door was left open and I listened to their conversation. The wife wanted something but it wasn't ready yet. "The size is unusual," the woman in the undertaker's repeated. "It must be ready soon," his wife said. I followed her back to their house.'

'Did you look inside?' asked Holmes.

'No. The curtains were closed. I waited for three more hours and then I saw two men arriving at the house with a coffin! Mr Holmes, what if the coffin is for Lady Frances?'

'Excellent work, Green!' said Holmes. 'Leave the rest to us… Watson, let's go! There is not a moment to lose!'

On the way to the house Holmes talked excitedly about the case.

'We have two possible options here, Watson: either she is alive or she is dead. Let's imagine they have sold all her jewellery. If she was still alive, she would go to the police so they'd have to kill her. If they want to bury her in a coffin, they'll need a death certificate. Did the doctor think it was a natural death? I'm guessing it was some type of poison. Or the doctor wasn't a real doctor… Stop the cab here, please!' he shouted to the driver.

ACTIVITIES

The text and **beyond**

PET 1 Comprehension check

Choose the correct answer — A, B, C or D.

1 Why did Holmes run to help Watson?
   A ☐ He didn't think he was doing a good job.
   B ☐ He was worried Watson would hurt the man.
   C ☐ He was worried the man would hurt Watson.
   D ☐ The maid was hurt by the strange man.

2 Why was the man looking for Lady Frances?
   A ☐ He wanted to convince her of his feelings.
   B ☐ He wanted to offer her a home in South Africa.
   C ☐ He thought she was going to marry someone else.
   D ☐ He wanted to take her back to England.

3 Why did Holmes ask about Dr Shlessinger's left ear?
   A ☐ The manager told him a criminal was staying in the hotel.
   B ☐ He didn't think Watson was taking the investigation seriously.
   C ☐ The Australian police asked him to look for an ear.
   D ☐ A criminal matching his description had a torn ear.

4 Who was Dr Shlessinger?
   A ☐ a man called Mr Peters who asks for money from wealthy ladies
   B ☐ a holy man who had a fight with the Australian police
   C ☐ a missionary called Mr Peters who was also a doctor
   D ☐ a man called 'Holy Peters' who looked after the dying

5 What did Mr and Mrs Peters sell?
   A ☐ They sold possessions they stole in South America.
   B ☐ They sold some valuable Swiss jewellery.
   C ☐ They sold a coffin at the undertaker's.
   D ☐ They sold some old Spanish necklaces.

6 What did Green see outside the house?
   A ☐ He saw Dr Shlessinger with a coffin.
   B ☐ He saw Lady Frances was inside the house.
   C ☐ He saw two men delivering a coffin.
   D ☐ He saw Dr Shlessinger's wife paying for a coffin.

53

ACTIVITIES

PET 2 Signs

Look at text in each question. What does it say? Mark the correct letter — A, B or C.

1. A ☐ Mr Smith can be contacted directly.
   B ☐ The undertaker lives in the shop.
   C ☐ Mr Smith can arrange services but not funerals.

Funeral Services
William Smith - *Undertaker*

w.smith@funeralservices.co.uk
Mob: 05842 627123

2. A ☐ Necklaces cost £20 today.
   B ☐ All jewellery is reduced by 20%.
   C ☐ Necklaces are cheaper today.

Hanson's Jewellers
Great 20%
discount on necklaces
today only!
WAS £20, NOW £16

3. A ☐ Tim is waiting at Flo's Cafe.
   B ☐ Christine will see Tim at the cafe.
   C ☐ The cafe is open until 1pm.

Hi Tim,
I've gone to Flo's Cafe.
I'll be there till 1pm.
See you there!
Christine

4. A ☐ You can contact the agency at any time.
   B ☐ All the detectives used to be policemen.
   C ☐ The agency has been open for twenty-five years.

Private Detective Agency
Police consultants with over 25 years' experience
24-hour service
Contact: 0806 568 9123

ACTIVITIES

3 News

Scotland Yard have been collecting information of crimes they think were carried out by 'Holy Peters'. Match the pieces of information (1-9) to a title (A-C).

A **Burglar arrested – Reverend Jones found 'not guilty'**
B **Reward for minister for catching the 'holy' thief**
C **Missionary steals fortune from South American heiress**

1 ☐ Miss Perez gave her money to a very good cause: the building of a church in Peru.
2 ☐ The minister fought with the individual and was able to take the statue from him, which he then kept safe in his house.
3 ☐ The reverend pulled out the knife used to kill his wife and killed the burglar.
4 ☐ The dishonest individual was a new member seen stealing a small gold statue.
5 ☐ Sadly, the missionary and his lady have departed and no church was built.
6 ☐ This explained the fingerprints on both bodies.
7 ☐ A burglar entered his house with a knife. On hearing his wife's screams, the man stabbed the unfortunate lady in the heart.
8 ☐ Anita Perez of Buenos Aires lost all her money to the wicked couple.
9 ☐ A minister helped the police with information about a man who came to his church.

Detective work

4 Decide which of these clues best matches each case in exercise 3.

1 ☐ He received a reward of 100 Australian dollars for his help.
2 ☐ The bank account for the church was false.
3 ☐ He received life insurance.

55

A C T I V I T I E S

Before you read

1 **Conversation**

Match the words Holmes says (A–D) to a response (1–4). Then match each response to the person speaking.

> Watson   Mr Peters   Honourable Philip Green

A ☐ 'You will be certain that I will find her...'
B ☐ 'Who is the lady in the coffin?'
C ☐ 'What time's the funeral?'
D ☐ 'Please look after Lady Frances...'

1 'Half past eight.' ....
2 'Thank you for all you have done.' ....
3 'You can't come in. You don't have a warrant.' ....
4 'She was my wife's nurse.' ....

2 **What happens next?**

A In Part Three you will read about a powerful <u>anaesthetic</u> called <u>chloroform</u> that is no longer used in medicine. Use a dictionary to find out what the underlined words mean.

B What do you think chloroform is used for in Part Three?

3 **True or false?**

Do you think these sentences are true or false? Listen to check your answers.

		T	F
1	Holmes shows Mr Peters a gun.	☐	☐
2	Mr Peters says he doesn't know Lady Frances.	☐	☐
3	There is an open coffin in the bedroom.	☐	☐
4	Holmes makes a mistake.	☐	☐

PART **THREE**

An Unusual Coffin

I knocked loudly on the door of the house. A pale, thin lady answered.

'I want to speak with Dr Shlessinger,' Holmes said.

'He doesn't live here,' the lady said.

Holmes put his foot in the door and held it open. A bald, red-faced man appeared. I knew straight away that he was the man we were looking for because I recognised his torn ear.

'My name is Mr Peters,' he said politely. 'There is no-one called Dr Shlessinger in this house. I think there must be a mistake, gentlemen.'

'I don't have time for this!' cried Holmes. 'If you're not the man I'm looking for, then I'm not Sherlock Holmes! Where is Lady Frances Carfax?'

PART **THREE**

'Mr Holmes, you say? I met a lady by the name of Lady Frances in Switzerland. She said she had no money. I paid her hotel bill and her ticket home. She gave me some jewellery in return. Unfortunately, it was worth nothing. I hope you find her,' he added in the same soft voice.

'You can be certain that I *will* find her,' said Holmes, '...in *this* house!'

'I'm sorry,' said Peters, 'you can't come in. You don't have a warrant.'[1]

Holmes showed him his gun. 'This is my warrant,' he said.

'Call the police!' Mr Peters shouted to his wife.

'Where is the coffin that came into the house today?' asked Holmes.

'Surely you must have some respect for the dead!' Peters cried.

Holmes and I searched the house. The coffin was in the dining room. Peters followed behind us.

'Open the coffin!' shouted Holmes.

'Never. I won't open a closed coffin!' he replied.

'Then I will,' said Holmes. He took out a knife.

'Watson, help me lift the lid,[2] please!'

We pushed up the lid and there at the bottom of a very big coffin was a poor old lady of ninety years old. Even I could see that she was not Lady Frances. Sherlock Holmes looked pale. He shut the lid angrily. Mr Peters was laughing loudly.

'Oh, I'd pay money to see that again! The man I've heard so much about — the great Sherlock Holmes — has made a mistake. Who did you think you were going to find: Lady Frances, perhaps?'

'Who is the woman in the coffin?' asked Holmes impatiently.

1. **warrant** : an official document that allows the police to search an area.
2. **lid** : top of a box or other object.

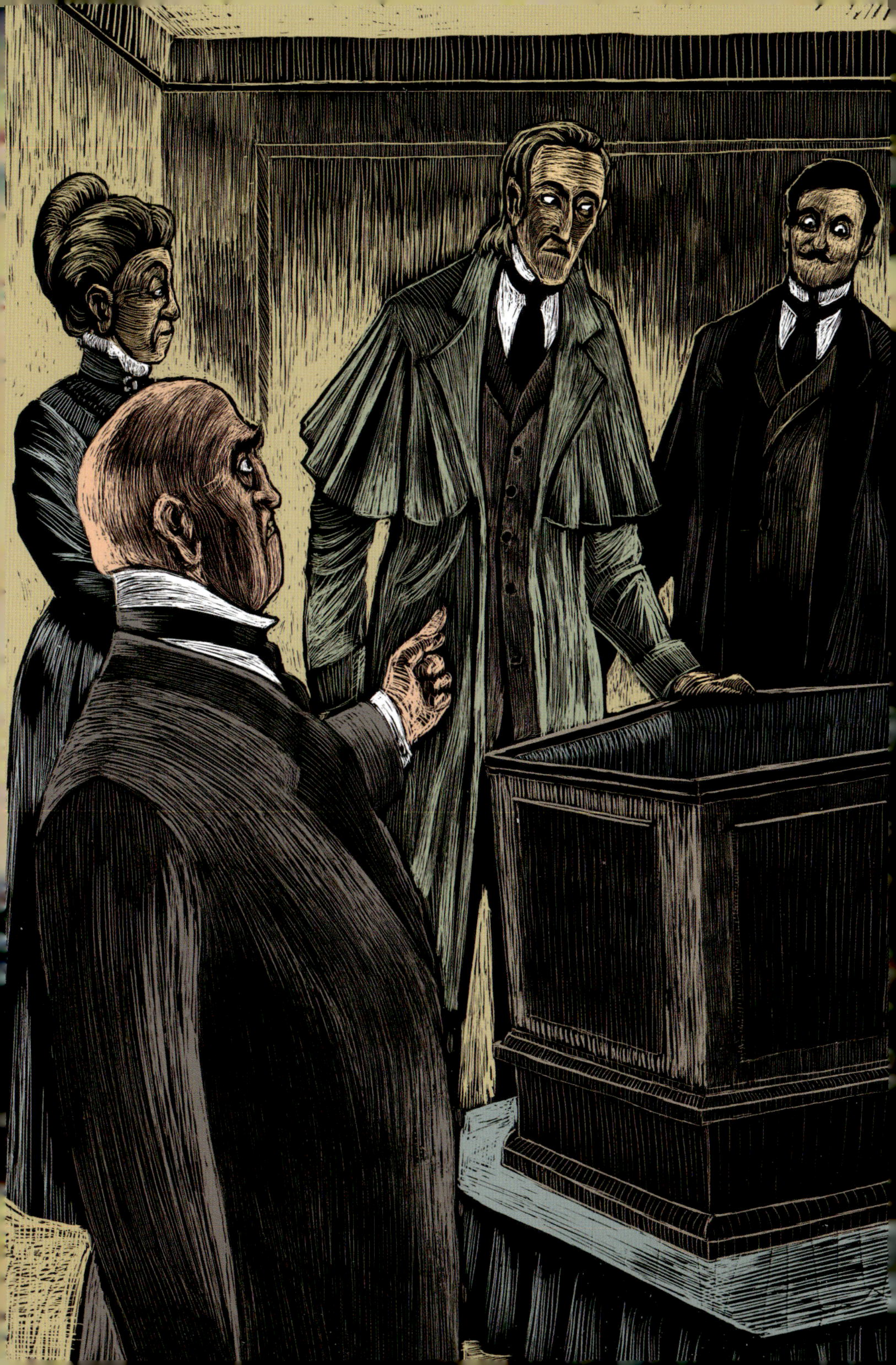

PART **THREE**

'We are kind people, Mr Holmes. She was my wife's nurse. She was very ill and she had no money to pay for a doctor so we looked after her in her final hours. She died a few days after she arrived. We paid for a coffin and we are going to bury her tomorrow. The funeral is at half past eight.'

Then we heard a voice behind us. It was the police sergeant.

'Holmes, I need to see your warrant.'

'Arrest him!' cried Peters.

We walked outside with the police sergeant.

'This matter isn't finished,' said Holmes. 'I will get a warrant. Watch these people carefully,' he added to the police sergeant. 'Don't let them leave the house.'

Later that day we went to Scotland Yard to ask about the warrant. When we returned I went to bed. I could hear Holmes walking around his room. He could not sleep. The next morning, at twenty past seven, he knocked on my door.

'Quickly!' he said. 'It's life or death, Watson, and very little chance of life! What time's the funeral?'

'Half past eight,' I replied.

Fifty minutes later we were at Mr Peters's house again. Four men were carrying the coffin to a carriage outside the house.

'Take the coffin back inside!' cried Holmes.

'Mr Holmes!' said Peters. 'Do you have your warrant or not?'

'The police are arriving with the warrant. The coffin must go back inside the house. I'll give a gold coin to the first person who opens it!'

Once inside, the men worked quickly to open it. I put my hand over my nose and mouth. The coffin smelt terribly of chloroform. Inside the coffin were two bodies and one of them was a pale but beautiful lady. Her head was covered in a cloth [3] left in

3. **cloth**: piece of material, e.g. from old clothes.

the anaesthetic. Holmes lifted her out of the coffin. At that moment the sergeant arrived with the warrant. Mr Peters and his wife ran out of the door. Two more policemen were waiting outside and ran after them.

'Doctor Watson, I need your help,' Holmes said.

Lady Frances was still alive. There was a small chance we could save her. Thirty minutes later, after some medicine and a lot of help to start her breathing again, she opened her eyes. She was very confused.

'You can take the poor old lady who is still in this coffin,' Holmes said to the men in the room. 'Maybe now she can rest in peace.'

We heard the sound of heavy footsteps on the stairs.

'Ah, I see the Honourable Green has arrived. Please look after Lady Frances,' Holmes said to him.

'Maybe in time, she will understand how much you love her.'

'Thank you for all you have done,' he said, taking the lady in his arms.

When we returned to Baker Street, Holmes was quick to discuss the details of the case.

'An intelligent man must learn from his mistakes,' he said.

'I thought about the case all night. I knew there was some clue… and there it was: the word 'unusual'. It's true. It was an unusually big coffin for a small body. They had a death certificate for the old lady. No-one would know their plan — they were going to bury Lady Frances alive so they wouldn't have to commit murder! I believe we found her just in time. These are very clever criminals, Watson. I'll be surprised if the police catch them. I'll be interested to see what they do next… very interested… What do you think? Should we ask Mrs Hudson for some tea?'

ACTIVITIES

The text and **beyond**

PET 1 Comprehension check

Decide if each sentence is correct or incorrect. If it is correct, mark A; if it is incorrect, mark B.

		A	B
1	The man who answers the door says he is Mr Peters.	☐	☐
2	Holmes shows his gun instead of a warrant.	☐	☐
3	Mr Peters's wife opens the coffin.	☐	☐
4	The lady in the coffin is an old lady.	☐	☐
5	The police sergeant gives Holmes a warrant.	☐	☐
6	Holmes offers a coin to whoever opens the coffin again.	☐	☐
7	Green helps to save Lady Frances's life with medicine.	☐	☐
8	Holmes says the police have caught the criminals.	☐	☐

2 Write correct sentences for the incorrect answers (marked B) in exercise 1. Then answer the following questions.

1 What did Mr Peters use before he put Lady Frances in the coffin?
2 Why was Watson able to help her?

3 Listening

Listen to the conversation at Scotland Yard and complete the warrant for the arrest of Mr Peters.

```
A warrant for the arrest of:
Name: .........................
Address: ...................
................ Brixton Rd
Reason: to ................
suspect is ...............
.............................
Date: ........  Time: ........
```

62

ACTIVITIES

4 Vocabulary
Put these words about health care in the correct group (1, 2, 3 or 4).

1 injuries	2 aches and pains	3 illness	4 treatment

stomach ache   ....   ear   ....
cough   ....   ache   ....
medicine   ....   cut   ....
sore knee   ....   back ache   ....
twisted ankle ....   cold   ....
injection   ....   bandage   ....
virus   ....   bruise   ....
wound   ....   flu   ....

T: GRADE 6

5 Speaking: health and fitness
Answer the questions with another student.

1 Is health care free in your country?
2 If you want to stay healthy, do you think it's better to see a doctor or to look after yourself?

Detective work

6 Read the case. Decide which of the sentences can/can't logically be true.

A magician is found dead in his own house in a large suitcase. The man lived in a block of flats with a porter. The suitcase is locked and the key is on a table. There are no signs that the man tried to escape from the suitcase. There is nothing in the room to suggest a stranger was there, for example, fingerprints.

　　　　　　　　　　　　　　　　　　　　　　　　　　　T　F
1 The magician killed himself and then got in the suitcase.　☐ ☐
2 The magician was trying an escape trick that failed.　☐ ☐
3 The magician locked the suitcase himself from the outside.　☐ ☐
4 Someone killed the magician and put him the suitcase for the concierge to carry.　☐ ☐

ACTIVITIES

PET 7 Comprehension check

Read the text below and choose the correct word for each space. For each question, mark A, B, C or D.

Buried alive!

The fear of being buried alive is perhaps one of the (0) ..C.. common human fears. In fact over the centuries, several objects (1) ..... invented so the victims of such burials could let people know they were (2) ..... alive. The first president of the United States, George Washington, feared being buried alive so much that he asked not to be buried until twelve days (3) ..... his death.

In *The Premature Burial*, the author Edgar Allan Poe describes the strange case of a woman found by the man she loved many years before. The man returned (4) ..... the village on hearing of the lady's death. Even though she had a husband, he decided to see his loved one just one more time. He went at night to open (5) ..... coffin where he planned to leave a piece of his hair. On touching her (6) ..... he saw she was still alive. He couldn't believe it and when the woman awoke she was amazed to see the man rescuing her was her old love. She didn't tell (7) ..... and the two left for America. Twenty years later they returned in the hope they would not be recognised. Her husband found out but the courts decided that in this unusual case she could remain with the man who rescued her.

0	A a lot	B more	(C) most	D bigger
1	A was	B were	C had	D has
2	A longer	B however	C still	D although
3	A later	B after	C near	D with
4	A to	B at	C in	D by
5	A it	B him	C an	D her
6	A hairs	B beard	C glasses	D eyes
7	A someone	B anyone	C it	D about

PET 8 Writing

Your English teacher has asked you to write a story (100 words). Your story must begin with this sentence:

The time I felt most afraid was when...

PART ONE

A Criminal Mastermind

Almost two years have passed since that terrible day. I never wanted to speak about it again but I feel it is my responsibility to describe the events leading up to it. A certain Colonel Moriarty, brother of Professor James Moriarty, is responsible for rumours and lies about the character of my dear friend Sherlock Holmes that I will not repeat here. I am the only one who knows what happened between Sherlock Holmes and Professor Moriarty and it is time that the world knew the truth.

    I still visited 221B Baker Street from time to time when Holmes wanted a companion to help with his investigations, but not as often as before. In the final year of my visits Holmes spent more and more time alone. The mystery he was trying to solve occupied a lot of his time but he wouldn't speak about it, not even to me.

PART ONE

One day, in early spring, I received a letter from France.

> Dear Watson,
> I am working in France for the French Government on an important matter that will take me many months to solve. The weather is good but the food is not so good. I hope all is well with the surgery.
> I will write again soon.
> Sherlock Holmes

From the letter it seemed clear that I would not see him for some time, so you can imagine my surprise when only a month later he appeared at the window of my surgery. He looked pale and very worried. He entered at a door around the side.

'I know what you're thinking,' he said before I could speak. 'I look terrible.'

I watched as Holmes went around the room making sure all the windows were locked. He closed the blinds.

'Holmes, what's the matter?' I asked.

'Air guns,' he replied.

'Air guns?'

'I think you know me by now,' he continued. 'I am not a nervous man but there's a difference between stupidity and courage, and when someone is trying to kill me... I don't want them to have a clear shot through your windows. Do you have anything to drink?'

I gave him a glass of water. He checked the windows again.

'I'm sorry for coming here so late. I won't stay long. I think it's best if I leave over the wall at the back,' he said.

'Holmes, please explain what all this is about.'

He said nothing. I looked at his hand. It was bleeding. I offered him something to clean it with.

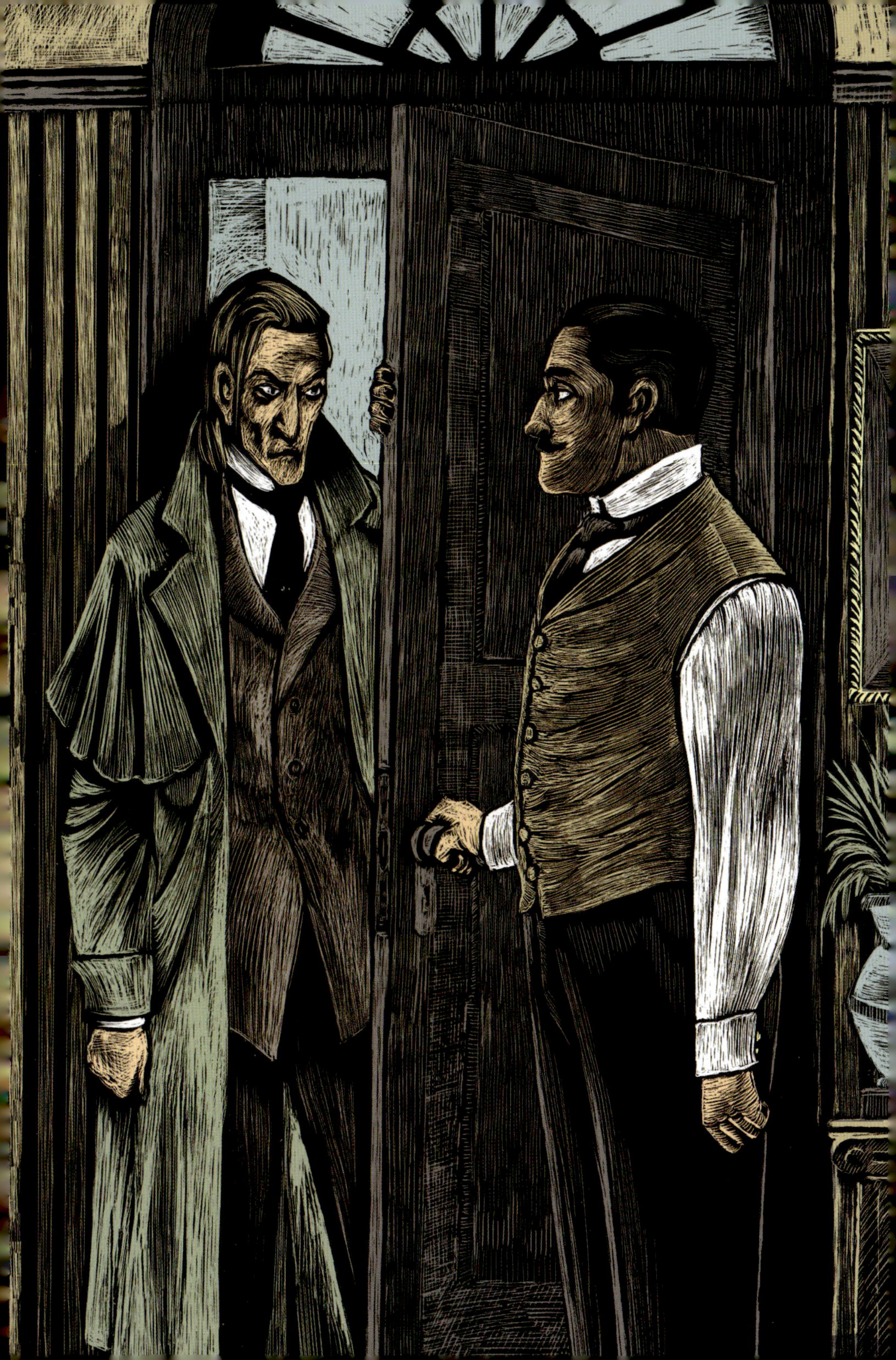

PART ONE

'Holmes, this isn't a little fight. Look at your hand!'

'Are you alone here in the surgery?' he asked.

'Yes, I am now. There is another doctor who helps me during the week.'

'Maybe he can help while you're away. I want you to come with me on a trip to Europe. I'm not sure of the exact location. We can decide when we get there.'

Holmes' behaviour was very strange. He never went on holiday. He certainly didn't go on 'trips' for no reason. He saw the worried look in my eyes.

'There's only one person I can trust with this information, Watson, and that's you. For the first time in my life,' he said, 'I have finally met my equal. His name is known to every criminal in London, but ask anyone in the street and they'll say they've never heard of him. Professor Moriarty! The man is a genius — he's a criminal mastermind!'

'Moriarty — a mastermind?'

'You see!' he laughed. 'No-one knows the real Moriarty — but I do! The man is responsible for half the crimes in London. I could continue working for the French government. It's a nice life, it's well paid, but I cannot rest until Moriarty is in prison!'

'Half the crimes in London!' I repeated. 'But if you really believe this, why haven't you asked Scotland Yard to arrest him? Do you have the evidence?'

'Crimes happen all the time. The criminal is caught. Sometimes they go to prison, then someone pays money and they go free. Sometimes they are never found. The important thing is that the man who controls everything is never caught. No-one must ever suspect him.'

The Final Problem

'But what does he do?'

'Everything and nothing! He is a well-educated university professor and one of the greatest mathematicians in Europe. At the age of twenty-one he wrote a thesis that was read all over the world. He was offered a job at a university. He worked very hard, but not towards anything good. He moved to London where he has chosen to use his extraordinary brain for a life of crime.

'No-one knows the criminal world better than I do. For years I have known that there is someone else behind the crimes I investigate. He is like a spider that sits in the centre of a very large web. He plans, he sits and he waits. He makes the threads and I follow them. In three days' time, with my information, they could arrest Moriarty and all his men. But if I take one step in the wrong direction, then all my work counts for nothing.

'I was sitting in my chair thinking about a case this morning, when a man walked into my room. I knew him immediately. His forehead was high, his skin was pale and his shoulders were round from the time spent in his study. His eyes were so dark I couldn't read the slightest emotion in them. He observed me with simple curiosity as his head moved from side to side like a snake.

'"You're not as intelligent as I thought," he said. "Don't you know it's dangerous to keep a loaded gun in your pocket?"

'I took out the gun that was in my pocket and put it on the table, but I kept my fingers close to it.

'"You know who I am," he hissed softly.

'If you have something to tell me, Professor Moriarty, I am free for around five minutes,' I replied.

ACTIVITIES

The text and **beyond**

1 Comprehension check
Complete the questions about Part One with the missing words and answer the questions. (You can use the puzzle in exercise 2 to help you.)

1 Who is called a .... mastermind?
2 Who is responsible for rumours and .... about Holmes?
3 Why is Watson .... when Holmes appears at the surgery?
4 By which .... does Holmes arrive?
5 What does Holmes close in the ....?
6 Does the man in the street think Moriarty is a ....? If not, what do they think he does?
7 How many .... does Holmes need to get evidence?
8 Why does Holmes say Moriarty is like a .... in the centre of a web?

2 Puzzle
Complete the puzzle with the missing words from exercise 1. The last letter of each word is the same as the first letter of the next word.

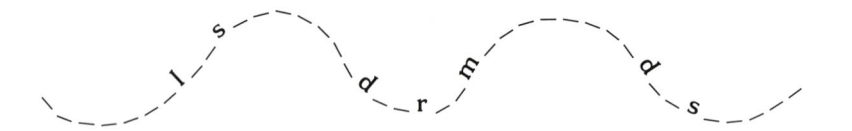

3 Moriarty
Use the information you know so far to help complete a profile of Moriarty.

Name: .... Moriarty ....
Occupation: ....
Experience: completed a thesis (subject ....)
Address: 33, Cheyne Court, ...
Description: ....
....

ACTIVITIES

PET 4 **Sentence transformation**
Complete the second sentence so that it means the same as the first. Use no more than three words.

0   Watson is the only person that Holmes can trust.
    ....*There is*...... only one person Holmes can trust and that is Watson.
1   Watson says he is the only one who knows the truth.
    Watson says .... else knows the truth, except him.
2   If Holmes makes a wrong move, his work counts for nothing.
    Holmes work doesn't count .... if he makes a wrong move.
3   Someone could shoot Holmes through the window.
    Holmes could .... through the window.
4   Holmes will be away from England for some time.
    Holmes .... in England for some time.
5   Moriarty is impossible to catch.
    No-one .... to catch Moriarty.

5 Animals
Which animals does Holmes compare Moriarty to?

Now match the following words with an animal (A–D).

1 ☐ web   3 ☐ scales   5 ☐ squeak
2 ☐ hiss   4 ☐ roar   6 ☐ mane

73

ACTIVITIES

Before you read

1 Conversation
Here are some sentences you will read in Part Two. Complete them with a word from the box, then put the sentences in the order you think you will read them.

| end | quite | danger | freedom | destruction | organisation |

A ☐ 'You are trying to take my ……………… from me.'
B ☐ 'There is a whole ……………… behind me.'
C ☐ 'I'd be ……………… bored.'
D ☐ 'I will happily accept my own ……………… .'
E ☐ 'Give me three more days and it will ……………… .'
F ☐ 'I'm not afraid of ……………… .'

2 Making predictions
Use your imagination to answer these questions about Part Two.

1 Can you guess who says the sentences in exercise 1, Holmes or Moriarty? Are there some sentences you think both could say?
2 Does Moriarty try to kill Holmes? How?
3 Do Holmes and Watson leave London? How do they travel?
4 Does Moriarty find Holmes?

3 Discussion
Make a list of questions to ask another student about what will happen next.

Does Moriarty try to shoot Holmes?

74

PART **TWO**

A Narrow Escape

Holmes moved around the room restlessly.

'And what happened next?' I asked.

'Moriarty asked me if I would continue with my investigations. I told him he already knew the answer.

'"Then you know mine," he replied. He put his hand in his pocket. I placed my fingers on the gun on the table but instead of a gun he took out a notebook and read aloud:

'"On the 4th January you passed me in the street, on the 23rd of January you were in my way, in the middle of February you were causing me problems, by the end of March I had to change my plans... Now I find, a month later, that you are trying to take my freedom from me. We both know that this cannot continue."

PART TWO

'You're right.' I said. 'It won't continue. Give me three more days and it will end.

'"You're an interesting opponent, Holmes. I don't know what I'd do without you. I'd be quite bored. You're smiling but I'm telling you the truth. This little game you are playing is too dangerous," he continued.

'I'm not afraid of danger. It's part of my profession,' I replied.

'"This is not danger!" he cried. "This is madness. There is a whole organisation behind me. Do you think you alone can stop it? There is only one end to this Holmes. We both know what it is."

'I enjoy your company,' I replied, 'but I have an important matter to investigate.'

'"I know every move you make. If you try to destroy me, I will do the same to you," he said.

'You are too kind if you think I am capable of destroying you, but I will happily accept my own destruction if I can free the world of you, Moriarty.'

'"Such a pity!" he said as he went out of the door, "but you leave me with no choice."

'Moriarty is a man of his word and he doesn't waste time. On the way here I almost lost my life three times. First, a carriage with two horses came towards me at full speed. Fortunately, I jumped from the road just in time. Then, as I was walking around the corner, a stone fell from the top of the town hall; it missed me by the smallest amount. Finally, on the road to your house a man attacked me. I hit him hard and he fell over.'

I was amazed at the way my friend spoke of these events. He was lucky to be alive and yet he told his story so calmly.

'You can understand now, Watson, why I shouldn't leave by the front door,' he continued.

The Final Problem

'Holmes, you can't go home. You must stay here!'

Holmes would not listen. He left, as planned over the back wall, but only after we had made arrangements for the next day.

'I'll see you tomorrow morning,' he said. 'Take this note. Follow these instructions carefully. Do exactly what it says. Destroy it afterwards.'

'Where will I meet you?' I asked.

'I'll see you on the train. The third carriage from the front is reserved.'

The next day I followed Holmes's instructions. I did not take the first cab that arrived outside my door, or the second, I took the third. I gave the cab driver an address to take my luggage to. I got out early, ten minutes away from the station. I ran around the corner where a horse and carriage was waiting. He didn't ask for my destination; he took me directly to the station. When I arrived I was just in time for the express train that connects with the ferry to France. I ran as fast as I could and I saw a porter taking my luggage to a carriage. There was a reserved sign on the window and I got in. There was a man in the carriage but it wasn't Holmes; it was a priest. I was confused. Holmes said the carriage was only reserved for us. I sat down and the train left the station.

Where was Holmes? After last night's events I was very worried for my friend's safety. Then the priest spoke.

'It's good manners to say "good morning," Watson.'

Within moments, I realised that Holmes, disguised as a priest, was sitting before me in the carriage.

'We must be careful. There's Moriarty now!' he added.

I looked out of the window and saw a man running towards the train, shouting angrily at the guard. I could see his large forehead

PART **TWO**

and small dark eyes in the distance. Holmes smiled, sat down, and took out a newspaper.

'Holmes, this can't continue. Tell the police they have to arrest Moriarty! They can hold him until you have all the evidence they need.'

'No,' replied Holmes. 'There are too many fish in this net[1] and I intend to catch them all. Now, we must plan what to do next. Moriarty will soon catch the train.'

'How?' I asked. 'This is the express train. There aren't any faster trains.'

'Think, Watson!' sighed Holmes. 'Moriarty is as intelligent as I am. Imagine I'm Moriarty! What would I do?'

'You could hire a private train.'

'Precisely.'

Fifty-five minutes later the train stopped at a station.

'Quick!' said Holmes. 'We're getting off here.'

'What about our bags?' I asked.

'They'll arrive in Paris, where one of Moriarty's men will wait for us to come and collect them. We won't be there, of course, because we're getting a ferry to Belgium. We'll buy new bags and new clothes on the way.'

We jumped off the train. Holmes pulled me to the ground and we hid behind some bags on the platform. I watched as the train left and our own luggage disappeared. At that same moment another train passed by on another platform, going at full speed. A man looked out of the window. We saw the face of Professor Moriarty.

'We guessed his plan,' said Holmes. 'We're lucky he didn't guess mine.'

1. **net**: material with holes to catch fish.

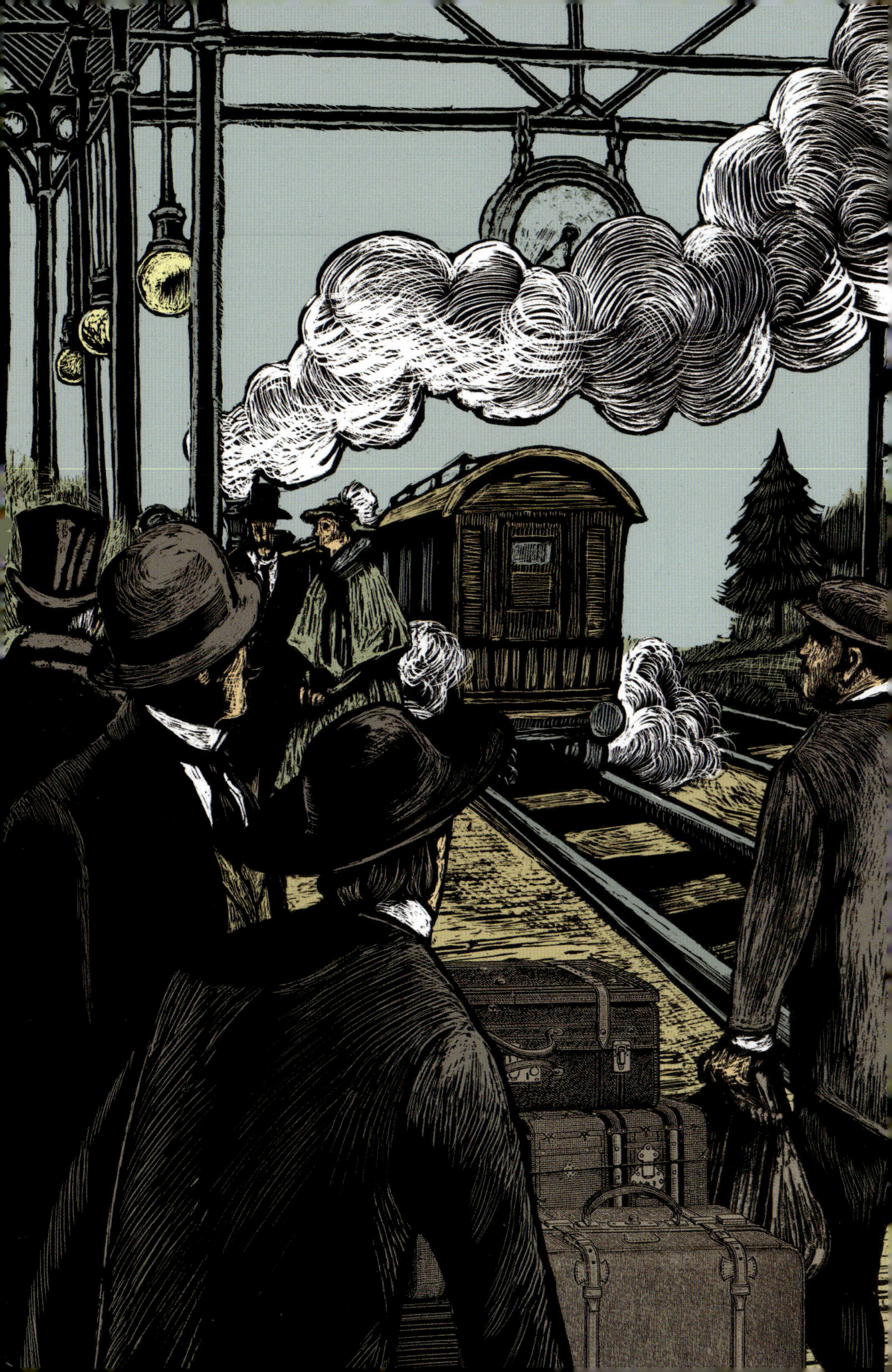

ACTIVITIES

The text and **beyond**

1 **Question words**

Choose the best question word and answer the questions.

| Where | Which | Who | What | How | Why |

1 ……………… does Moriarty take from his pocket?
2 ……………… is Watson amazed that Holmes is so calm?
3 ……………… does Holmes leave the house?
4 In ……………… carriage must Watson meet Holmes?
5 ……………… is the priest on the train?
6 ……………… are Holmes and Watson going to get a ferry to?

2 **Writing**

Complete the summary of the events that happen between Moriarty's visit to Holmes and Holmes arriving at Dr Watson's surgery.

1 *He was almost run over by…*   2 *A stone fell…*   3 *A man…*

3 **Instructions**

Rewrite Holmes's instructions to Watson in order. Use full sentences.

Take the carriage waiting outside the flower stall on Green Park Rd.

Carriage waiting outside flower stall: Green Park Rd
Third carriage from front reserved
Third cab (no other)
Get out: Hyde Park Corner
Luggage: cab driver with address
Best not be late!

ACTIVITIES

4 Listening

Listen to the advertisement for a train service and complete the poster at the train station.

FAST TRAINS TO EUROPE

1 Fast check-in .... departure.
2 Food and drink ....
3 Travel from .... direct.
4 .... with plenty of leg room.
5 .... in the Business Lounge.

T: GRADE 5

5 Speaking: means of transport
Answer the questions.

1 How do you prefer to travel to:
   - get to work/school?
   - go on holiday?
2 Do you think it is better to travel by train or plane? Give reasons.

Detective work

6 Look at some of the things forensic scientists do discuss how a forensic scientist might help you in the cases 1-3.

- Examine bodies and record information; use chemistry to examine the evidence.
- Identify people using fingerprints; crack codes.

1 A man was found in his study. There was a lot of blood but no sign of entry.
2 A couple were found dead in the kitchen. There was no sign of any injuries.
3 Someone has been kidnapped. Their computer was still on.

Sherlock Holmes in *Popular Entertainment*

Early adaptations of the Sherlock Holmes stories

When Sir Arthur Conan Doyle first wrote the Sherlock Holmes stories they were published in a magazine in instalments.[1] This way of telling stories in parts was perfect for the theatre and later for radio, film and television. The earliest plays of the Sherlock Holmes stories were already appearing during Conan Doyle's lifetime. Conan Doyle even wrote a play himself. This play was completed with the help of the actor William Gillette and was a big success in the theatres of America and Britain. In the play, Gillette played the character of Holmes. He wore a hat called a 'deerstalker' hat and smoked a large curved[2] pipe. Although in the books Holmes didn't wear a particular hat or smoke this type of pipe, the image of the famous detective with his hat and pipe has become known all over the world.

By the 1930s many homes had a radio and by the 1940s the radio was one of the most popular forms of entertainment. Many radio actors played the character of Holmes including Orson Welles. Over the years people have listened on the radio to nearly all the Sherlock Holmes stories and they are often repeated. There are also new adventures written especially for radio.

1. **instalments** : a story divided into parts. (You see or read these each week/month to find out what happens at the end.)
2. **curved** : not straight.

Television

Holmes and Watson help the police but they don't work for the police. In some ways they work outside the law. The longest series to appear on television was in the United Kingdom and ran from 1984 to 1994. This series starred[3] the actor Jeremy Brett as Sherlock Holmes and Edward Hardwick as the loyal and clever Watson.

There have also been some more modern adaptations. The BBC TV series *Sherlock* (2010-2012) shows a detective living in London today. He sends texts and he uses the Internet to help him solve crimes – and he never wears a hat! In a new American TV series, *Elementary*, Dr Watson is a woman and Holmes and Watson live in modern-day New York.

Film

One of the most recognisable actors to play Holmes was Basil Rathbone. He played Holmes in fourteen films from 1939 to 1946. His version of Holmes was a polite, well-dressed gentleman who never did exactly what the police or the criminals expected.

More recent films have tried to make us see Holmes in a different way. In the films by the English director Guy Ritchie – *Sherlock Holmes* (2009) and *Sherlock Holmes: A Game of Shadows* (2011) – Holmes doesn't just defeat his enemies with his mind and his powers of deduction, he

3. **starred**: had a role as the main actor.

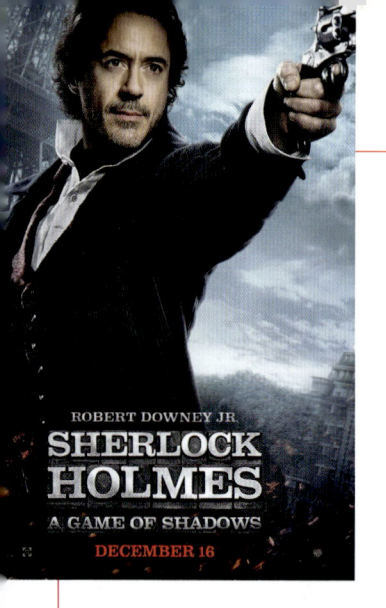

defeats them with his fists[4] and his abilities in martial arts[5] as well. At first, the new Holmes does not seem to match the traditional image – he looks untidy and he is slightly mad – but in many ways he is not as different from the Holmes in the original stories as many people think. The real Holmes often did behave in strange and unusual ways. Holmes showed he was able to fight in *The Valley of Fear*. He also mentions his abilities in a Japanese martial art called 'baritsu' in *The Adventure of the Empty House*.

Maybe it is possible then to see Holmes not just as one man but as many different faces of one character: Sherlock Holmes has many disguises. One thing remains certain, Holmes is just as popular today as he was when Conan Doyle first introduced his readers to the world's only consulting detective, and the stories are sure to entertain audiences for many years to come.

① Comprehension check

Match the sentences to a form of entertainment.

          a play   **b** radio   **c** television   **d** film

1 ☐ Holmes uses his abilities in martial arts to defeat his enemies.
2 ☐ William Gilette appears in a 'deerstalker' hat.
3 ☐ Orson Wells played the character of Holmes and Moriarty.
4 ☐ A modern Sherlock sends texts to his friend Watson.

4. **fists** : your hand is referred to as your fist when you have bent your fingers in towards the palm in order to hit someone, to make an angry gesture or to hold something.
5. **martial arts** : traditional sports from Asia; a way of fighting.

ACTIVITIES

Before you read

PET ① **Listening**

You will listen to the first part of Part Three. Tick the picture closest to the answer.

1 What (or who) came down the mountain?

A   B   C

2 Where did Holmes and Watson stay?

A   B   C

3 Where did the guest house owner suggest they went?

A   B   C

② **Vocabulary**

The word 'falls' is an abbreviation for which word?

85

PART **THREE**

The Reichenbach Falls

On the third day of our travels in Europe, Holmes sent a telegram to the police. Later that evening he received a reply.

'I knew it!' he cried.

'Have they caught Moriarty?' I asked.

He shook his head. 'He has escaped. You should return to England, Watson. Moriarty will try to find me.'

'No,' I said. 'I'm going to come with you.' We discussed the matter for over an hour until Holmes became bored and agreed that I could stay.

Holmes decided it was best for us to walk from France into Switzerland with the help of a local guide.

One day, after days of walking, we sat down on a pretty area of

THE FINAL PROBLEM

grass to eat. I looked up and saw a huge rock falling from the top of the mountain towards us. I jumped out of the way and pushed Holmes to one side.

I was surprised the guide didn't try to help. He told us coldly that rocks often fell from the mountain. It was wise to be careful.

'Who's there?' I cried. I ran up the hill, but there was no sign of anyone.

Holmes decided to change our plans. We took a different route into Switzerland and we left our guide. Finally we crossed over the Alps. We arrived at a small village where we rested at the guest house. The owner spoke good English. He knew London well from his time there in one of the city's finest hotels. He told us about the sights in the area.

'You really must go and see the Reichenbach falls,' he said. 'They are a beautiful sight at this time of year. You should stay another night.'

We said we had no plans to stay longer; and that we would continue to the next village of Rosenlaui, but Holmes agreed that we should see the falls first as we weren't far away.

After more than an hour along a steep, narrow path, we heard the falls. The water from the melted snow from the mountains fell into the depths below with a sound like thunder.[1] The path ended at the waterfall. The only way back was along the same path we came. Smoke seemed to rise from the black rock at the bottom like a cauldron.[2] I shouted to Holmes who was at the end of the path; I heard the echo of my voice from the bottom of the falls. We rested on a rock near the falls to admire the view.

1. **thunder**: loud noise heard during a storm.
2. **cauldron**: large round metal pot used on an open fire.

87

PART **THREE**

Soon after a young Swiss boy came running towards us with a note in his hand.

'Herr [3] Doctor!' He shouted to me. He handed me the note. It was written in English.

'*A young English woman is very ill. We think she is dying but she doesn't speak any German. We need an English doctor to come quickly before it's too late.*'

Holmes agreed he would continue to Rosenlaui with the Swiss boy as a guide. I would find another guide and see him later. I went back down the hill as quickly as I could to see the poor woman.'

'Where's the patient?' I asked. 'I hope she's not worse.'

'What do you mean?' the guest house owner asked.

I handed him the note written on hotel paper.

'Didn't you write this?' I asked.

'No,' he said. 'This is very strange.'

'Can you remember anyone asking you for paper?'

'Not long before you left a well-educated Englishman came here…'

I didn't wait to hear any more because I knew the rest. When I was coming down the path to the hotel, I remembered seeing a man on the other side of the hill walking up towards the falls. He was tall and thin and… I ran back up the path, but it took longer to go up than to come down. When I arrived Holmes wasn't there. My worst fear was true. There wasn't a sick English lady. It was all a lie so that I would leave Holmes.

I tried to think what Holmes would do. It didn't take long to find out what happened. The sight of Holmes's walking stick against a rock nearby told me that his journey went no further than the end of the path by the waterfall. There were no footprints returning back towards the path. I could see the torn roots of plants, and

3. **Herr**: a title for 'Mr' in German.

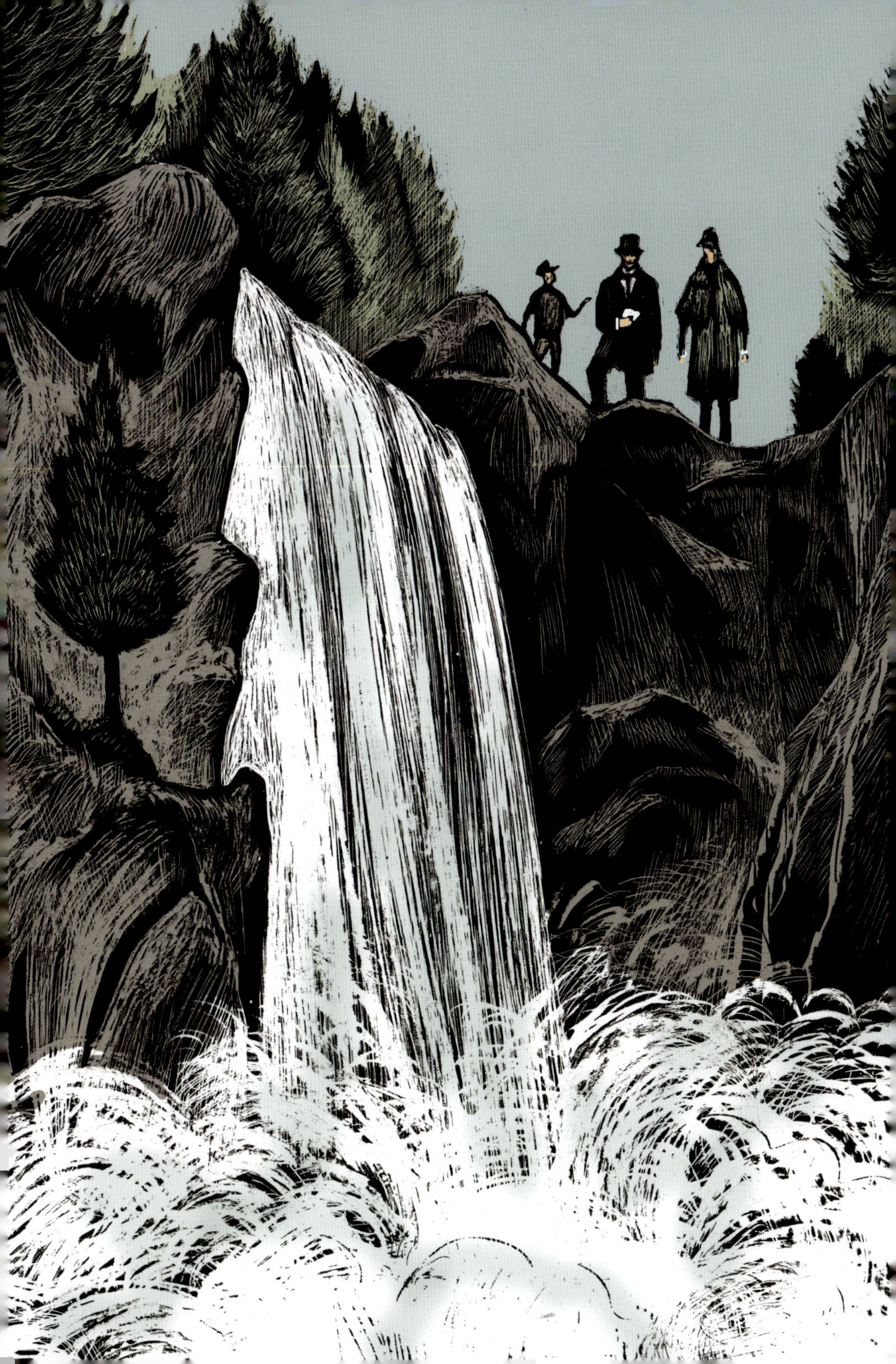

PART THREE

finally the mark of a long fingernail in the ground at the edge of the falls. I looked over into the black water beneath and shouted as loudly as I could.

'Holmes! Sherlock Holmes!'

'Sherlock Holmes!' came the echo of my own voice. I shouted again but it was no good. In that cauldron was one of the world's most dangerous criminals, and in my stomach I knew my friend and one of the world's greatest detectives was with him until the end.

Then, on the rock next to the walking stick, I saw a small silver case. I picked it up. There was a note inside. It read:

> I am grateful to Professor Moriarty for giving me this opportunity to write to you. Now I will finally defeat one of the world's greatest criminals. Tell everyone the news. The police have all the information they need. I have left a file with my brother Mycroft.
>
> I am sorry, Watson, because I know this will be particularly difficult for you, my dear friend, but my disappearance from this world is the price I must pay.
>
> Yours truly,
> Sherlock Holmes

Then I understood the guide was paid by Moriarty and Holmes was left alone for the final battle with Moriarty, which ended, so the local police say, with both men falling to their deaths in the falls. The information Holmes left with the police was enough to send most of Moriarty's men to jail but little was ever said of their leader, which is why I feel it is my duty to speak of it now.

I cannot replace the emptiness that has been left in my life but maybe Holmes was right: his disappearance was the price only a brilliant detective could pay. Sherlock Holmes was, and always will be, the best and wisest man that I have ever known.

ACTIVITIES

The text and **beyond**

PET 1 Comprehension check

Decide if each sentence is correct or incorrect. If it is correct, mark A, if it is incorrect, mark B.

		A	B
1	The police were not able to arrest Moriarty.		
2	Holmes doesn't want Watson to come with him.		
3	Holmes doesn't trust the guide taking them to Switzerland.		
4	The guest house owner could only speak German.		
5	Holmes and Watson plan to stay a few nights at the guest house.		
6	The Swiss boy wrote a note about a sick English lady.		
7	Holmes left his walking stick against a rock near the waterfall.		
8	The police caught Moriarty's men with Holmes's information.		

2 Breaking news

Read the newspaper article about the events at the Reichenbach Falls. Find at least six facts that are different from Watson's story and correct them.

DAILY NEWS

FAMOUS CONSULTING DETECTIVE IS KILLED

Today the body of the famous Scottish detective, Mr Sherlock Holmes, was found after he fell from the top of the Reichenbach Falls. The detective left a small gold case at the hotel where he was staying with his assistant Dr Watson and a note for his brother, Mycroft Holmes. The police in London are looking for a young German boy. It is thought the hotel owner paid the boy to push Holmes from the Falls. A friend of Colonel Moriarty is also said to be missing.

91

ACTIVITIES

③ Your holiday review

Read this information from a website where tourists can write reviews about their trip. Think of somewhere you have visited recently and write a short review for a website.

> ★★★★
> A lovely town in a beautiful part of Switzerland. The Reichenbach Falls are worth a visit. There were lots of references to Sherlock Holmes but I wasn't really that interested in him!

PET ④ Listening

You will hear a tour guide giving information. Complete the information in the numbered space.

Sherlock Holmes tour in Meiringen

Visit to Meiringen
- See the (1) .... of Sherlock Holmes
- A chance to take (2) ....
- Visit the Sherlock Holmes (3) ....

Lunch
- Choice between fondue or steak and (4) ....

Excursion to Reichenbach Falls
- Take the (5) .... on the funicular railway
- Tour finishes at (6) .... p.m.

'Holmes agreed that we should see the falls first.'

When we use **should** we mean that in our opinion it is a good thing or the right thing to do.

We can also use *should* to say something we expect to happen.

The train should arrive at nine o'clock.

Should is a modal verb. It is followed by the infinitive (without *to*).

You should return to England.

ACTIVITIES

5 Should

Holmes has noted some things he thinks will happen. Use *should* to make new sentences for the examples below.

1 We arrive at the falls at 2 p.m.
2 Moriarty is there.
3 Watson finds my note if I don't survive.
4 The police are able to arrest the criminals.

Detective work

6 You are all experts in crime solving but you look at things in different ways. Pick a colour below and take the view of the person connected with that colour.
Then answer the question:

Is Holmes dead or alive?

- This person takes the positive point of view. They think of the best thing that can happen.
- This person takes the negative point of view. They think of the worst thing that can happen.
- This person is the creative thinker. They think of an imaginative answer that sounds impossible.
- This person is the logical thinker. Their answer is based on the facts they know.

Examples:
- No-one saw Holmes's body so he could still be alive.
- Yes, but there are no footprints on the path going back.
- Maybe he found an air balloon.
- But where would he get an air balloon?

93

AFTER READING

1 Picture summary

Look at the pictures from the three stories. Write the correct title and a suitable caption under each one.

A

B

C

....
....
....

....
....
....

....
....
....

D

E

F

....
....
....

....
....
....

....
....
....

AFTER READING

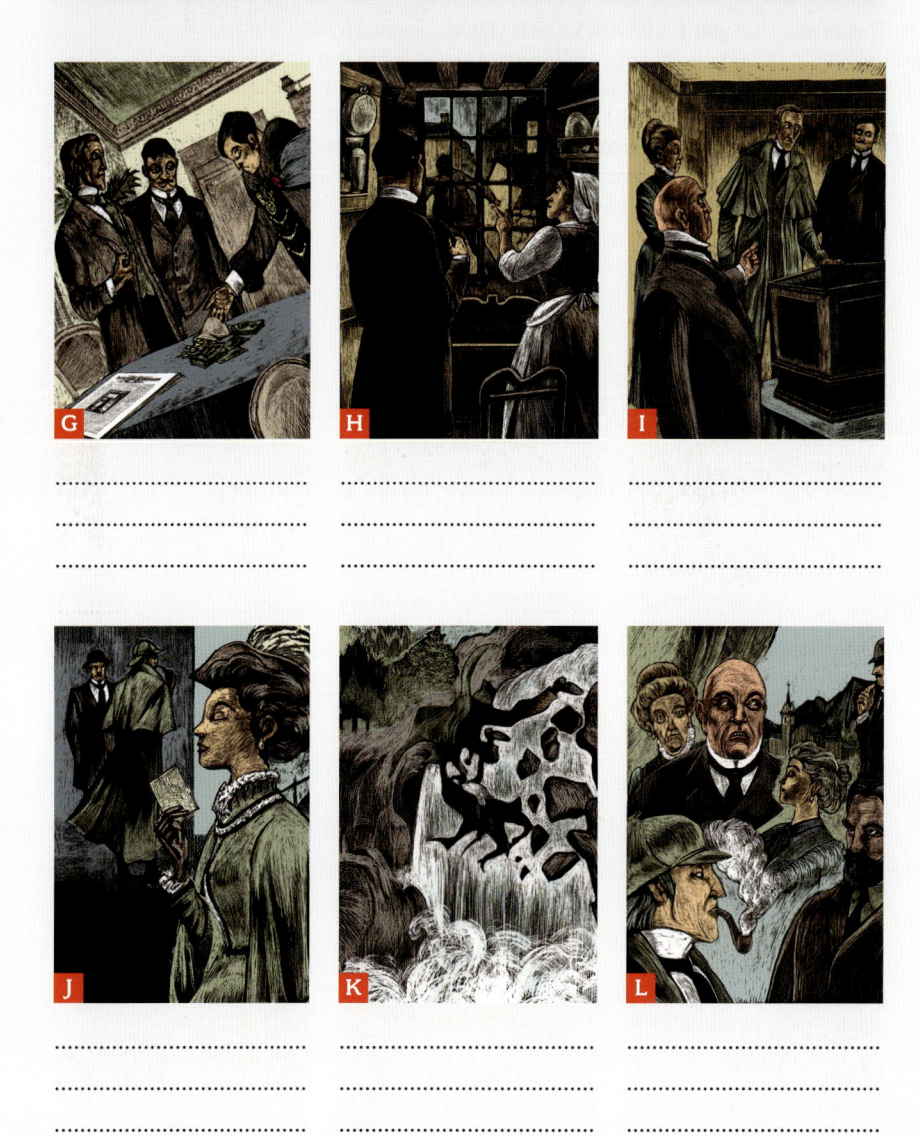

G

....
....
....

H

....
....
....

I

....
....
....

J

....
....
....

K

....
....
....

L

....
....
....

This reader uses the **EXPANSIVE READING** approach, where the text becomes a springboard to improve language skills and to explore historical background, cultural connections and other topics suggested by the text.
The new structures introduced in this step of our **R**EADING & **T**RADING series are listed below. Naturally, structures from lower steps are included too. For a complete list of structures used over all the six steps, see *The Black Cat Guide to Graded Readers*, which is also downloadable at no cost from our website, www.blackcat-cideb.com.
The vocabulary used at each step is carefully checked against vocabulary lists used for internationally recognised examinations.

Step Three B1.2
All the structures used in the previous levels, plus the following:

Verb tenses
Present Perfect Simple: unfinished past with *for* or *since* (duration form)
Past Perfect Simple: narrative

Verb forms and patterns
Regular verbs and all irregular verbs in current English
Causative: *have / get* + object + past participle
Reported questions and orders with *ask* and *tell*

Modal verbs
Would: hypothesis
Would rather: preference
Should (present and future reference): moral obligation
Ought to (present and future reference): moral obligation
Used to: past habits and states

Types of clause
2nd Conditional: *if* + past, *would(n't)*
Zero, 1st and 2nd conditionals with unless
Non-defining relative clauses with *who* and *where*
Clauses of result: *so*; *so ... that*; *such ... that*
Clauses of concession: *although*, *though*

Other
Comparison: *(not) as / so ... as*; *(not) ... enough to*; *too ... to*